How Do You Find the Time

How Do You Find the Time

By Pat King

Illustrated by Edna Haavik

AGLOW PUBLICATIONS
Edmonds, Washington

Acknowledgments

I wish to express my appreciation to my husband Bill, who constantly supported every aspect of the writing of this book; to Jo Anne Sekowsky, who lovingly and painstakingly critiqued every word; to Katie Fortune, who never lost the vision that this book would exist; to John Sherrill and through him, Eadie Goodboy, who provided much of the background; to Father Dennis Bennett and the Reverend Wayne Butchart, who reviewed it for scriptural accuracy; to Marianne Wingfield, who heroically typed the first draft; to Bette Stautz for typing the last draft; to the generous *Aglow Magazine* typists, Susan Blacksten, Barbara Peterson, Bev Chamberlain, Dorothy Deppa, Charlotte Bowles, Janette Lane, Angie Schiermeyer and Lois McGrew, who gave hours of their time; and finally my deep appreciation to the many women who so willingly shared their own experiences in finding enough time.

TABLE OF CONTENTS

1
The
Beautiful
Clipper

There is enough time. I discovered this wonderful truth quite by accident at a time when my marriage was crowded with children and the idea of enough time seemed as remote as enough money and as elusive as Ponce de Leon's mystical fountain of youth. I discovered it in phases and by making mistakes. But I know now, most certainly, that each of us has been given abundant time, more than enough to do everything we have been called to do in this life.

How do we find it? There is no single answer or magical cure-all. How handy it would be if we could close our eyes, turn around three times, say "abracadabra" and immediately solve our personal time problems. How convenient it would be if we could just read all there is to read about time and, when we were finished, miraculously do all that we had intended to do for the past few years.

To be expected, the answer is not that easy. But there is a way to find enough time. The way is challenging and it can be delightful fun. As you discover it, you will get to know a lovely person better than you have ever known her before. She is you and, together as we go through this book, you and I are going to have a marvelous time.

Let's begin by picturing a card table set up in your front

room with a jigsaw puzzle partly started on it. In the middle, someone has pieced together a beautiful clipper ship, so stately it is almost regal. As the wind propels it along, its sails billow out like a hundred petticoats worn by a princess majestically gliding into the center of a grand ball.

In a corner of the card table are the azure and white and lightly tinted blue pieces of the puzzle that make up the sky and its soft floating clouds. In another corner are the deep aquamarine pieces of the water. In still another corner of the table someone has sorted out all the rich brown green pieces of the land. There are still a few pieces scattered about that don't seem to belong anywhere but you get the feeling, as you look down at the card table, that there will be a stunning picture when all the pieces are fitted together.

This book on time is that jigsaw puzzle. The pieces of the sky that form the backdrop are the overall principles of time management. They are absolutely necessary and, when pieced together, they are quite impressive by themselves, but they are still not the total picture. The aqua-colored pieces are the deep support of a life-style that must flow in the harmonious order that God has called us to, if there is to be enough time. The rich browns and greens of the land represent the down-to-earth planning that must be done with the Lord's help before the sailing can begin.

Of course, the ship, the beautiful belle of the ball, is you. The wind that billows your sails, guides you and sets you on your course is the mighty and yet ever-gentle wind of the Holy Spirit. Without it, you can put the picture together but the beautiful clipper will have no power.

As you read this book let the pieces fit around you. Interlock the sky and water and land, the principles of time, the necessary order and the planning to form a perfect frame for you. The unique way that you will take the pieces and maneuver them around into something that is right will result in an *objet d'art* that is not just "suitable for framing," but is your own original masterpiece. The Holy Spirit will sail you into new and undreamed-of adventure as you enter, at last, a place where there is enough time.

2

The Not-so-Catchy Slogan

My own discovery, the place where I first learned the principles of time management, began in a little ranch house on a street unimaginatively called Twelfth Avenue. I was young, twenty-five, with six children under eight years of age. My husband Bill was a young executive who worked a great deal of overtime. And overtime for Bill meant that the burden of the children was mainly mine. I had grown up in a relatively small family: my parents, my sister Wanda, a year younger, and my brother Ralph, six years younger. Now, here I was with more children than I had ever dreamed possible (and more to come). Even though I loved them with all my heart, the burden of caring for them was overwhelming.

Still, I might have been able to blunder along and make it somehow, day after day, until they reached school age, except for one painful complication in my life: an eighteen-month-old complication named Johnny. If Johnny had behaved, if he hadn't cried constantly and pulled at my legs, demanding my attention every waking moment, I could have managed on my own steam.

But, as it was, Johnny and I had climbed aboard a grim carousel of frustration. His constant crying slowed down all the other work and made me furious with him. My fury made him cry and his crying made me feel guilty until a horrible animosity grew between us. The more this animosity grew, the more Johnny cried, and around and around we went. He was thin, so thin his dark eyes seemed to be his whole face and he was pitifully woebegone.

Doctors hadn't been able to diagnose Johnny's condition but it had been suggested that his crying was psychosomatic. Then one day in July a new doctor, young Dr. Fong, took a long time examining him. Finally, he stood back and said in a voice that did not seem quite positive, "This little fellow looks like one of the starving children I've seen in China. It could be that he has an ailment that keeps him from digesting certain foods and, this in turn, gives him severe stomach cramps and causes him to cry." He wondered if I had ever heard of celiac disease.

So it happened that the answer to Johnny's crying was a strict diet that eliminated wheat and other foods that were anathema to him. But the answer to Johnny's sad little personality was not so easily found. He needed attention, lots of it from me. So on top of all the housework every day there had to be time sandwiched in between a new baby and four other children for one little sad-faced eighteen-month-old toddler who had forgotten how to smile. Fortunately, it didn't occur to me to ask for help from family or friends or I might never have learned what I did, for those months of struggle laid the groundwork for all the years that were to follow.

Dr. Ted Engstrom of the *Managing Your Time* seminars has a name for what I learned, actually a slogan that he uses to teach the principles of time management. He calls it *goals, priorities, planning*. First, one must decide what she wants to accomplish. These are *goals*. Then, she must establish which are the most important and these are the *priorities*. Then, she must decide how to get them done and this is the *planning*.

In that little house on Twelfth Avenue, without knowing the slogan, I set a goal — to see Johnny smile. Dr. Engstrom says that goals should be measurable so that you can tell when you have attained them. My full goal was to keep on giving Johnny attention until he smiled. It had top priority, the one thing that could not be cut. I needed to plan how it would be done. So, in my groping desperation, I had stumbled upon one of the great resources of enough time.

The planning began. Obviously, meals had to be prepared and cleaned up after, clothes had to be washed, housework had to be done, and the other children's needs met. But, by getting up at 7:00 a.m. and by keeping it simple, I could do this work by 10:00 each morning. From 10:00 to 12:00 became Johnny's own special time. After naps, from 3:00 to 5:00, became all the children's time with Johnny's needs foremost. I don't remember all the games, puzzles, books and songs we did together, but I do remember that it was hard.

I was just beginning to learn about the committed Christian life and I was discovering two things for sure: without the strength of the Lord, keeping such a schedule couldn't be done and that all things are possible through Him. Sometimes I ended up in the bathtub or in church (the only two places where I could be alone) and prayed, "Jesus, You carried that heavy cross for me; please help me to carry this heavy burden of a sick baby for You." I knew it was His continuous support that carried me through each day.

It took three months before Johnny gave me a little half smile, but the problem of emotional illness was only scratched so I set another goal — to keep on with Johnny's special time until he smiled so broadly I could see his dimples. Every day, even on Sunday and vacations, with the Lord's ever-present help, I planned for Johnny's time.

A year went by and still no dimples. It was July. We were at the beach where the family had taken a cottage for two weeks. Together, Johnny and I walked along the edge of the surf, he, balancing on a log, I, beside him. Something tender had happened to our relationship in this year: the animosity was gone and I had grown to love him in a special way.

This day, as he came to the end of a log, he said, "Jump." I held out my arms. As he jumped, he smiled, a smile so grand that both of his dimples sparkled in his cheeks as brightly as splashes of sunshine on the water. I held him closely and let the tears of relief and happiness fall. It had taken a whole long, hard year, but that smile was worth it all.

Johnny's complete recovery took another ten years, including concentrated prayer for his total healing. But the beginning, the most important phase, had happened because the Lord had led me into the principles of time management.

It's easy to see how I can appreciate Dr. Engstrom's three-word slogan. I've used it over and over from planning a company dinner to taking my turn at jury duty. But many women have said it works even better with one more word. That word is *purpose.*

Another way to say it is this: *before we set our goals or make our plans, let's know what we want.* Do we want to start our own TV talk show? Do we want to start a prayer group or teach a religious education class? Do we just want to be better Christians, better women or better mothers? Or do we just want a day to ourselves? Whatever it is, letting the Lord help us is the beginning step while Dr. Engstrom's three specialized words and our additional one comprise the guideline. As a slogan it's bulky. It would be awkward at a football rally, but for the sake of accomplishing our dreams, let's start saying it: *purpose, goals, priorities, planning.*

I'm sure that each of us could put together a long list of things that need doing. Some lists are orderly and others are mentally wadded together and pushed into our subconscious in the same way that undesirable leftovers get pushed to the back of the refrigerator. There was an Erma Bombeck column in the evening paper in which Erma wrote of the woman who made her feel so inferior because she ironed everything including belt buckles and zippers. Erma confessed that her own ironing bundle had been mildewing in the back of the refrigerator for several years.

Surely, every woman who read that column identified with Erma. We all have been waiting to do or intending to do many things that we haven't gotten around to. We say we could do them if we just had more time.

Some of us need time for our families; others need time to earn a living. Many women today need time for both. We need time for our parents and time for our community and time to be creative. It's that awkward four-word slogan that is going to help us. Women who have found enough time all seem to practice this; they have known their purpose and developed their goals, priorities and plans.

Uncle Ralph and Aunt Lilly live on the other side of the state and I doubt that they have ever heard of time principles. Yet those principles have allowed them to do something that many others cannot find time for. They have a son, my cousin Kenneth, who is so severely retarded that even at age thirty-seven he has never learned to speak. In twenty-five years they have missed only one monthly visiting day at the institution where they reluctantly placed him. To Aunt Lilly it's simple: "He is our son and we want to see him *(purpose)*. So on visiting Sunday, we drive out there after church *(goal)*. No matter what comes up, we put it first *(priority)*. It's simply a matter of not working it into our schedule, but working our schedule around it *(planning)*. And it's important to him, too," she added. "On the one Sunday we were back East and didn't come, the staff was amazed to see him crying and looking for us since Kenneth understands so little."

The principles of time management were a key to a changed life-style to my friend, Charlotte, a single parent. When she finally sent the last of her four children off to seek his fortune in the world, she took a hard look at the next twenty years ahead of her. The work of raising a family alone had taught her the joy of giving and she knew the time ahead would be frustrating if she could not give herself to it as fully as she had given herself to her family.

Although she had never attended college, her purpose became a college degree in special education with particular interest in working with the deaf. Her source of revenue gone (child support), she worked in a department store to support herself. Using her earnings to attend night school, she was able to take one subject each quarter while she saved money to attend school full time. By trusting in the Lord, while at the same time giving single-minded attention to her priorities and plans, she graduated *magna cum laude* at age forty-seven. Today, a full life beckons her from many directions. What she had learned of purpose, goals, priorities and planning carries over into her innovative work with the handicapped.

The same principles have helped other women to do the impossible. In *The Hiding Place* Corrie ten Boom tells how she and her sister, Betsie, were incarcerated in the infamous German prison camp, Ravensbruck. They, and the women with them, suffered from atrociously cruel guards, torturous roll calls in freezing weather and, literally, a starvation diet. There, in the filth and disease, where whistles and loud-speakers planned their day, Betsie and Corrie prepared for the future beyond their prison walls.

Betsie was given a vision of a home where they could care for and love both prisoners and guards to show them that love is greater.

> It's such a beautiful house, Corrie! The floors are all inlaid wood . . . and gardens! Gardens all around it where they can plant flowers. It will do them such good, Corrie, to care for flowers!

Before their dream could be an actuality, Betsie died in prison, but Corrie, back in her native Holland, was given the very place that Betsie had seen and fulfilling the dream became Corrie's purpose. In June after the war many people arrived there . . . "silent or endlessly relating their losses, withdrawn or fiercely aggressive, everyone was a damaged human being." Corrie's goal was to help them back to wholeness. "It [healing] most often started as Betsie had known it would in the garden."[1]

For Corrie, seeking the good of the whole operation became her priority. Her plans meant giving up her own comfort and continually putting up with difficult people. But reaching her purpose, the realization of Betsie's and her dream, was worth it all.

We can use these principles for ourselves by looking inward and taking stock. These are times when we come to understand that there is another step to take in our Christian walk. This happens over and over, despite all previous spiritual progress. Augustine said so long ago and so well:

> Our hearts, O Lord,
> Were made for Thee
> And restless ever will they be
> Until they rest in Thee.

Even in this situation of spiritual need Dr. Engstrom's slogan can be applied through prayer. "Lord, my purpose is to live in complete union with You. Show me how You would have me live and let that be my goal. Give me the grace to make that goal my highest priority and supply me with wisdom as I make my plans."

And so we have a beginning. The area of our lives where we use Dr. Engstrom's time-management slogan corresponds to the pieces of azure and white and lightly tinted blue of the puzzle. So far there's not enough to give an idea of the picture that is forming before us. Let's get started on what we do have and work those pieces into something that fits a problem corner of today's search for enough time.

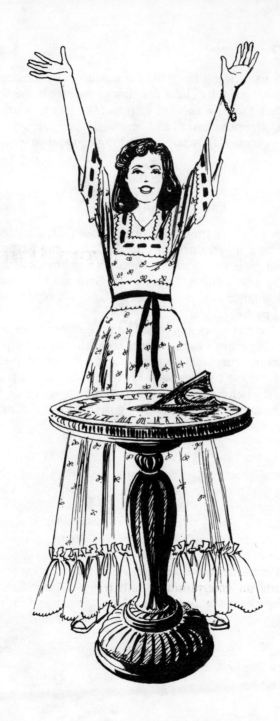

3

Time for Everything

Recently, a financial advice column in the newspaper told of a young couple without children who together earned $63,000 a year. The story interested me primarily because this young couple, unable to live on their combined salaries, were deeply in debt. They made exorbitant house payments, furniture payments, car payments, boat payments, insurance payments, charge account payments and, in addition, spent large amounts on entertainment and travel. The columnist recommended that they turn their salaries over to a firm that would budget for them and teach them to spend their money wisely.

After reading this article I put the paper down and tried to imagine how I would spend $63,000 a year. Even after the school and orthodontist bills were paid in full, it seemed there would still be an enormous amount left over. I decided, as I'm sure nearly every woman who read the column did, that I would manage very well on that much yearly income.

I feel the same way about time, and I would like to suggest that *we can have even more time than that couple had money,* more than enough time coming to us yearly, thus enabling us to manage everything in our lives we've been called to do. God who is the creator of time is also the giver of time. God always gives lavishly. Even a cursory look at creation tells of His generous hand. The sky is filled with uncountable stars in our own galaxy and beyond that is another galaxy and beyond that, enormous other galaxies extending into space far beyond the comprehension of human minds. God is so lavish that one pine tree has within its cones the potential for beginning 100,000 new pine trees a year. Our own reproductive systems are bountifully endowed by the Creator. Between the ages of fifteen and forty-five most women produce 390 ova, each one of which, if fertilized, could begin a new life. Multiply that by the millions of women in their childbearing years throughout the world and we are staggered at the overwhelming provision for new life God has made.

Since God is a generous God, it makes sense that He has given us time in abundance for everything He has called us to do. Let's look at the familiar discussion on time in Ecclesiastes:

> There is a right time for everything:
> A time to be born, a time to die;
> A time to plant;
> A time to harvest;
> A time to kill;
> A time to heal;
> A time to destroy;
> A time to rebuild;
> A time to cry;
> A time to laugh;
> A time to grieve;
> A time to dance;

A time for scattering stones;
A time for gathering stones;
A time to hug;
A time not to hug;
A time to find;
A time to lose;
A time for keeping;
A time for throwing away;
A time to tear;
A time to repair;
A time to be quiet;
A time to speak up;
A time for loving;
A time for hating;
A time for war;
A time for peace.

(Eccles. 3:1-8 TLB)

Truly, there is a time for everything, time in abundance. Jesus, who is ever our example, never appeared rushed. He was very tired at times. He was sorrowful at times, even discouraged, it appears, but He was never in a frantic hurry. For every person He healed, thousands never met Him and so remained unhealed. For every person He taught, thousands did not hear His teaching. Yet He did not hurry. We never hear Him say, "There is not enough time for My work." He had come into the world for one purpose, to save the world, but He did not take it upon Himself to be more or to do more than the Father asked.

God who is the creator of time gives time to us to use for His purposes as extravagantly as He gives His other gifts and as certainly as He gave His Son enough time to do His work. Then why don't we have enough? Why are we always looking for more? Why do we say, "If only I had more time?" We would have liked to ask the young couple making $63,000 a year, "How are you using your money? Are you spending it on things you don't need?" Perhaps we can ask ourselves, "How am I spending my time? Am I spending it on the unnecessary? If I were to do some changing would I have more than enough?"

We've already heard that *knowing our purpose is the key to getting our work done.* So perhaps we could begin to answer these questions about how we spend our time by finding out what our purpose is. One of the biggest religious sellers is a novel that deals with this theme. Even though the story is outdated the book is still being sold and read. The success of Charles Sheldon's *In His Steps* is not in its script but in its message. It deals with a minister and the members of his congregation who, before making every important decision, ask themselves, "What would Jesus do?"

This question is still as fresh and as illuminating as the dawn stretching its fingers out across each new day. To make it easier to apply to our generation and to our quest for time, we can ask ourselves an updated version, "What is my purpose? What has Jesus called me to do with my time?"

I had never considered the question carefully until I heard Al West, the late editor of *Logos Journal,* talking to a group of Christian writers. He pointed his finger at us and said, "All of you may think you have been called to write, but I say to you, that is not your calling."

He paused and the room was so still the low hum of the air conditioner became a noisy irritation. I wondered, as I supposed many others did, what could he mean? We were all writers; certainly we were called to write. Al continued, "You have been called to follow Christ. If you are a writer, then that's something you do along the way."

I'm not sure what else he said because my mind was back on "called to follow Christ." Called to follow Christ! Yes, I had known that since I'd been eleven years old at summer camp and learned to sing at the top of my lungs, "I will make you fishers of men if you follow Me." But this night I began to truly consider it for the first time.

When I asked myself the question, "What is my purpose? What has Jesus called me to do with my time?" the answer came: *follow Him.*

Practical application, however, wasn't as simple. At home, away from the pointing finger of Al West, I sat at the kitchen table with a baby on my lap. While he smeared his teething biscuit on the wall I wondered, "How does a woman with a job or a family to get off to school or little children under her feet all day, or a husband to always consider, follow Jesus?"

Heaven only knows the work a woman must do, the interruptions she lives with and the people who usurp her time. When I had belted out that song at summer camp I'd pictured myself a missionary in some strange country teaching the Bible to an open-air classroom of intent children. But that was surely impossible now. Clearly, for me to follow Jesus didn't mean for me to dump what I was doing and rush out to the mission field.

But what did it mean? What could it mean to me, a woman, a wife and a mother, a chauffeur, a cook and a housemaid? What did it mean to the Christian woman anywhere who wanted to find enough time to do all that must be done in a day or a lifetime? It sounded like I was adding just one more thing to an overbusy schedule. Yet the words of Jesus were there in the Bible, "If you refuse to take up your cross and follow me, you are not worthy of being mine" (Matt. 10:38 TLB).

I washed the teething biscuit off the baby, the table, the wall and my arms and thought about the Scripture verse. All that day and for many more weeks and months I pondered how I would find the time to follow Jesus. Then, slowly, slowly, as I began to consider these things we have just talked about, it at last occurred to me that if God who is the lavish giver of time has called us to follow Jesus, *then there will be enough time to do everything He has called us to do.*

And so I began to understand that to obtain this lavish gift from the Father I had to first know my purpose. And that purpose was to follow Christ and glorify Him. The goals, priorities and plans that followed this realization were as old as time itself. For they meant simply finding God's order for my life.

I discovered that following Christ with the order in our lives God intends us to have does bring all the time we need. I

hope you will come along through the next few chapters and
see for yourself. I am not an expert, but a person like you who
needed enough time. Hopefully my failures and discoveries,
the commands of Scripture and the experience of others on
the same quest will help to guide you, too, to that delightful
place where there is in your own life, abundant time.

4
First
Things
First

There is a story told of a bishop who had the heaviest work load of any priest in the diocese. He was a good man, a holy man, they said, and it was well known that he rose at five o'clock in the morning and spent two hours in prayer before his day began. All the different organizations and groups he spearheaded prospered spiritually and materially.

However, many of the younger clerics thought the old man was overworked and secretly wondered when he would cave in from exhaustion. Their surprise was great when a conference of bishops gave him, in addition to his other duties, the responsibility of coordinating the overseas missionary society. He threw himself into that work as if he were a young man and that society prospered like everything else under the old man's ministry.

One day his colleagues could bear it no longer. Taking him aside, they asked him his secret. "How could you possibly take on such a large project without sacrificing just a bit here or a bit there of your other duties?"

The old bishop looked amazed at their question. "Why, the answer is simple. The more I have to do the more I pray. I rise an hour earlier in the morning for prayer and everything else I must do during the day just seems to mind itself."

How he learned this I never heard. But it seems safe to guess it was from the Scriptures, for Jesus Himself gave the words and the example. He was talking to the people who followed Him and recognized Him as a great teacher because He spoke so compassionately to their concerns. We can picture Him standing in the midst of these ordinary people, every eye riveted on Him.

> And why worry about your clothes [He counseled]? Look at the field lilies! They don't worry about theirs. Yet King Solomon in all his glory was not clothed as beautifully as they. And if God cares so wonderfully for flowers that are here today and gone tomorrow, won't he more surely care for you, O men of little faith? So don't worry at all about having enough food and clothing. Why be like the heathen? For they take pride in all these things and are deeply concerned about them. But your heavenly Father already knows perfectly well that you need them (Matt. 6:28-32 TLB).

Then, I imagine that Jesus paused and looked each member of the crowd in the eye so each would understand the importance of what He had to say next. "[The Father] will give them to you [all of these things you need] if you give him first place in your life and live as he wants you to" (Matt. 6:33 TLB).

Just as surely as Jesus was speaking to people and to their needs then, He is speaking to us and our quest for time today. If we give Him first place in our lives and live as He wants us to live, He has promised to give us all that we need.

Not only did Jesus tell us we can trust God for everything when we put God first, but He gave us the example through His actions. One particular morning His disciples woke up at the usual time and found Him gone. He had spent the day before preaching, healing, walking and mixing with the people who closed in on Him. His disciples yawned and stretched and said to one another, "He is no doubt close by. We'll just look for the nearest crowd and find Him there."

But everywhere they went the crowds who had gathered to see Jesus asked them, "Have you seen Jesus of Nazareth today?"

At last Simon found Him out in the wilderness alone, praying to His Father. "Come," Peter said, "everyone is asking for You."

Jesus replied, ". . . We must go on to other towns as well, and give my message to them too, for that is why I came" (Mark 1:38 TLB).

He knew what was ahead of Him that day. He had three options: one was to get some badly needed sleep and trust that the Father who had sent Him on His mission would give Him the strength and the time. The second option was, in view of all that had to be done, to get up early and get going; the third was to take time to be alone with His Father before His work began. Of the three, should we choose less than He did?

Yet, praying seems difficult at times. Leila, my young neighbor, said, "I know I should take the time to pray, but when I do make time for it I can't get started. Then I end up thinking about other things or else falling asleep. And not only that but I'm such a sinner, I can't face God."

Many of us, like Leila, make prayer too complicated. The children have a simple definition of it that should be enough for all of us. They call it "talking to God." We grown-ups like to remember that prayer consists of adoration, contrition, petition and thanksgiving. The children tell us that prayer is, *"I love You, I'm sorry, please help me, and thank You."*

I like the children's version best and Leila did too when we talked about it. When we are standing in the middle of the floor or sitting at the kitchen table or kneeling in the bathroom it helps to have a prescribed way to turn off the concerns of the day and turn to prayer. If our minds go blank after the "Here I am, Lord," then we can remember how the children do it.

Why not pray: "I love You, Father. I love You, Jesus. I love You, Holy Spirit. I love You and praise You because You are so lovable and so worthy of love. I love You and praise You because . . . " (Each of us can add her own reasons for loving and praising. Psalms 145-150 can help us until we get the knack).

"I'm sorry. I'm sorry about the mean thing I said yesterday to Annie. I'm sorry about giving in to temptation to gossip. I'm sorry about not telling Sarah about You. Please forgive me, Jesus." (We know that we are forgiven because the Bible tells us we will receive whatever we ask for in Jesus' name. We also know that Jesus' death took our sins away [1 John 4:10; Col. 1:14]. As Leila and I and millions of women before us have found out, we can be forgiven of our sins and, as their ugliness is washed away, they no longer stand between us and our conversation with the Father).

"I need something, Lord. Please give me the love I need to be kind to Annie. Please give me the strength to turn away from the temptation to gossip. Please give me the courage to tell everyone who asks about You. Also, Father, the boys need tennis shoes this week. Will You provide them? And Bill needs Your help at the meeting. And Father, I need to get everything done on today's list."

And then, in conclusion . . . "Thank You for loving me. Thank You for forgiving me. Thank You for the courage and the tennis shoes and the help and the time."

Of course, this only scratches the surface of prayer. Volumes enough to circle the globe, I'm sure, have been written on it. There are many readers who have gone beyond wondering where to begin when the moment for prayer comes. There's prayer in tongues, there is mental prayer, there is listening prayer, and on and on. There is a daily offering to God of our lives, which we'll come to later. But for those who draw a blank at prayer time, the four types of prayer can be a springboard to a wonderful experience. If that kind of praying makes us feel childlike, then so much the better, for Jesus told us we must become as little children.

Irene Harrell tells us in her book *Prayerables* how she discovered that she must put prayer first. It seemed that she wanted to begin typing before she prayed. But as she began, the first paper had so many mistakes that she had to start over; the second one was put in backwards, and the third paper was put in with a wrinkled carbon. She stopped, paused, and reflected. Yes, perhaps there had been time to pray first, after all.[1]

Denise Adler is a woman of wealth, of many skills, talents and friends. She is perhaps best known as a teacher of the Bible. We sat in her lovely living room. A fire crackled in a massive fireplace while foghorns sang a hoarse melody from the bay beyond her window. Her first book *Morning Star* was just out and Denise talked of it and her love of the women she teaches. It seemed to me that I was in the presence of a Christian who had everything. Here was a woman of material wealth as well as a woman with a sense of Christian well-being.

"And what about daily prayer first thing in the morning?" I asked her, knowing full well the answer.

Yes, she agreed that this was the way to start the day. And then she added, "And it's a good thing I do or I would never see any growth in my life. You see, I tell my classes you can't come into the presence of God through prayer and remain the same person. Just the other morning I experienced this anew myself. I went to pray as one kind of person and left that period of prayer as a totally different woman."

She told me she had been reading Catherine Marshall's book *Something More* the night before and read about the dangers of holding resentment towards others. The author had urged her to forgive all those who had wronged her, but instead of doing this, Denise had turned the pages and kept on reading.[2]

On the following morning she began praying as usual when the challenge of Catherine's book came to her mind so strongly that there was nothing left to do but face it. Denise Adler, the Christian who looked as though she had everything, saw a part of her life that she had never dealt with before, the whole area where she held resentment against others. For an hour and a half she prayerfully wrote down those feelings of resentment she harbored against her various family members, then she forgave each one. She summed it up, "It was a wonderful relief to me and a great joy to be freed from that resentfulness, but I never would have done it unless I had taken the time for daily prayer."

Let's give this matter of daily prayer the benefit of Dr. Engstrom's time-dispensing slogan. (Every time we use his time-management principles, we can add a few more azure pieces to the background of the sky in our puzzle.)

The *purpose* of prayer is to do as Jesus did and to take Him literally when He admonished us to seek first the kingdom of God. Our *goal* should be daily time alone with the Lord. The *priority* we give it should set it ahead of everything else in importance. The *plans* we make for prayer time should be realistic enough that they can be carried out at a time when no one needs us: first thing in the morning, as soon as the family is gone or right after the baby lies down for his nap.

Sometimes we are tempted to excuse ourselves from this daily time of prayer by saying, "Well, I'm a Martha, not a Mary, and that's the way it is." Yet, we know that this is only an excuse and a flimsy one at that.

Although it may be difficult at first, eventually prayer becomes a joy. There comes a time when we no longer do it because Jesus tells us we must seek God first, but because there is nothing else we would rather do. There is a woman in our church who spends many hours sitting in the pew just looking at the altar. When our old pastor asked her if she was praying she said with a smile, "Oh, my, no. I'm just sitting here enjoying Jesus and He is enjoying me."

For now let's continue our search for enough time by planning a place for prayer in our lives. In the picture forming before us the most beautiful and vibrant colors are the ones of prayer we are now just fitting together. They form the water around the hull of the beautiful clipper. The deeply colored aqua pieces of prayer are what give support to the beautiful ship as she sails along.

Without prayer we can, of course, still sail but only at our own speed. With prayer and its supportive water flowing around us, there is no end to the adventures beckoning us onward.

5

Something Worthwhile

One evening Bill and I left the house right after dinner in order to see our lawyer about an important matter. I told the children that, although we hated to leave them alone at that time of night, we had to see the lawyer before their Dad's trip. I asked their help with the evening work. "Will you do the dishes?" "Will you get the baby ready for bed?" "Boys, will you please take care of the mess in the rec room?"

When we arrived home two hours later, the dinner dishes were still on the table, as yet untouched by human hands. The baby was still in his grubby bathing suit and the mess in the rec room had multiplied. Bill marshalled the troops into the kitchen and demanded to know why the requests for help had gone unheeded.

Two of the culprits hemmed and hawed and finally admitted they had been watching TV, trying to get themselves off the hook by insisting that it had been educational. But it was one of the girls, the one who was supposed to be bathing the baby, who gave the most incredible response. Self-righteously she excused herself with, "You know that little girl up the street that nobody likes? Well, I decided to play Monopoly with her like you are always telling me I should."

"But your mother told you to get the baby ready for bed."

"Yes, but she also told me to be kind to the little girl."

"And what were you supposed to have done first?"'

A chastised voice at last answered, "The baby."

Obviously the children had neglected what they were supposed to do with the excuse that something else to their liking was more worthwhile. Perhaps this is a common failure of mankind. I wonder how many of us women are guilty of the same kind of misdirected decisions in our roles as wives. We are called to marriage and so often we put that calling last because something else is educational or meaningful or charitable. Hannah Whitall Smith puts it this way:

> When we appoint a servant for an especial part of the work of the household, we want him to attend to that alone, and not run all over the house trying to attend to the work of all the other servants. It would make endless confusion in any earthly household if the servants were to act in this fashion, and it makes no less confusion in the Divine Household.[1]

At a Christian family conference the speaker told this story:

> A young woman, Polly, a pastor's wife, came to see me about her time problems. She was so discouraged she sat at my desk and held her head up with her hands. "I don't know what's the matter with me," she said. "I can't get anything done. There was a time when I just loved taking care of my husband and being with him and supporting him in his work. Now I'm so far behind I dread it when he comes in weary and wants part of my already spoken-for time."
>
> I talked first about purpose. Did she have one? Did she know what her calling in life was? She was certain she had it straight, God first, helping in her husband's church second, family third.
>
> As we talked of right order she saw, yes, God had called her to be a woman who put time with Him first. But He had called her to be a wife to her husband second, not only a wife who kept his home flowing peacefully so he

could save his energy for his work, but a wife who had time to sit with him when he was weary, admire him when he was discouraged, make love to him when he needed her.

As we talked Polly could see that this kind of home life would do more for her husband's ministry than any of her organizing or piano playing. She saw that, third, she was called to be a mother to her little girl and that the church and all the activities there should actually be fourth place in her life.

She went home to try and work it out with the promise she'd come back in a month and discuss it again. Even though she saw what right order should be she doubted she could do it because everything was so set in the opposite way. We prayed that day for help beyond her own. "Father, please give Polly the wisdom she needs to get her life in right order and give her the courage to do it."

In two months a new Polly returned, the conference speaker reported. She didn't have to prop her head up. Instead she had a new vitality. She said that she hadn't done anything at first except pray that God would show her what to do. And He did. She found herself getting replacement people for all the jobs she did in the church except pianist in the children's Sunday school. Next, she found that without the burden of so many church activities her housework was no longer undone.

But it was her marriage that was so exciting to her. At first she felt almost sinful because she wasn't doing something every minute. However, her husband showed her that he desperately needed some of that time. As she used this time to sit with him, love him and make love to him he had new energy for his work. She said that truly without doing anything in the church, she had greatly enlarged her husband's ministry. Their little girl noticed the change, too, and quit telling people that her mommy "lived at the meeting."

It was the new order in her life that made the new Polly: kingdom of God, *first;* her husband, *second;* her family, *third;* and the church and community after that.

When we said our marriage vows we promised to forsake all others for this person we pledged our lives to. When my friend Irene was reminded of that promise she did a remarkable thing. Irene was one of those wonderful Christian women in demand as a speaker and teacher. Her husband, Mike, was one of those so-so Christians who went to church but took no part. Irene hoped that he would become a leader some day, but of course she wouldn't dream of interfering. "After all," she said, "Mike becoming a leader has nothing to do with me. That's between God and him."

One morning when the children were off to school and Irene was kneeling for a time of prayer she began to realize that God had something important that He wanted her to hear. She sensed that He was going to open up to her a new ministry. She cried out, "Oh, Lord, whatever it is, I'm Your willing servant — use me." Then she heard the words in her heart that were almost unbelievable, yet she was absolutely sure of them. *"I want you to be Mike's wife."*

"But I *am* Mike's wife."

She heard again in reply, "I want you to be Mike's wife."

She got up from her prayer corner and wandered around the house. It didn't seem fair. She was a good homemaker and she knew it. She baked and cleaned and canned and sewed and decorated and she was faithful. Of course, she was Mike's wife.

Taking an Amplified Bible off the shelf, she opened it to Ephesians 5:22:

> Wives, be subject — be submissive and adapt yourselves
> — to your own husbands as [a service] to the Lord.

She went over the words again slowly. Did she really love Mike? Did she put him first, did she honestly revere him? Painfully, she began to see herself as the servant girl in Hannah Whitall Smith's book who had been called to one part of the household and was, instead, overseeing the work of another part. She was "everything" to the Christian community but, and it took courage to admit it, she wasn't "everything" to Mike.

Irene has always been dramatic, throwing herself totally into whatever she does and, for that reason, she is a good example only because of what happened in her life. All of a sudden, almost overnight, she dropped every one of her outside activities and began to spend most of her time in her home. When the church called for a teacher or a friend called and asked her to lead a prayer group she declined. No matter what came up she turned it down so that she could be a 100 percent wife to Mike. In the evening she sat with him, watched TV with him, jogged with him (which she hated), played cribbage and, most importantly, frequently made love to him. A year went by, a hard year. Irene had laid down her life and it required continual sacrifice. Mike continued as a so-so Christian. I kept in long-distance contact with her and she often confided that she felt as though she were walking in a dark valley. She greatly missed being thought of as a women's leader, but she was determined to be nothing more than a wife to Mike.

Another year passed, this one harder than the first because her friends, not knowing her reasons, began to tell her that her refusal to lead and teach was selfish. Some even said that they had a word from the Lord that she was supposed to be a teacher or a Bible leader.

A couple of times during the second year Mike was called on to lead a devotion. He did it badly, at least she thought so, and she wanted to show him how. But he didn't ask her advice and she knew that love doesn't give unwanted opinions. She kept on making love to him, jogging and playing cribbage.

Then in the middle of the third year, something stirred in Mike. God began calling him, and he answered that call. Slowly Irene began to realize that if she had remained the sought-after, advice-giving spiritual authority in their Christian community, Mike would have been too threatened by her success to venture out. For two-and-a-half years more she remained "only a wife" to Mike. In that time Mike changed into the Christian leader Irene had always dreamed of his becoming. Today, at Mike's insistence, they teach young married couples together. Now it's the team of Mike and Irene who are in demand as speakers.

The story, of course, doesn't end there. As "Mike's wife" Irene began enjoying a love from him she hadn't known before. Their children, their friends, even acquaintances all say they experience a great peace in her home they hadn't felt before. One woman said (and it was quite a suprise because the children had misbehaved so much that day), "I've never known such peace anywhere as I've felt in your house. If that's what Christianity produces then I want it." So the circle of people Mike and Irene touch as a couple widens and widens. They don't play cribbage any longer because Mike's newfound ministry keeps him too busy. Irene still dislikes jogging, but she enjoys making love to her man more than ever.

Admittedly, although true, this is an extreme example. Some may not feel called to do anything outside their home for five years. Some may be so far from the life-style of Irene that they can only shake their heads in amazement at her. But, basically, all can learn from her; she gave her time over to being a wife and a great blessing has come to her household.

My efficient and organized friend, Evelyn, made an interesting chart that was suggested at a Christian conference. She made a column of everything she had been called by God to do and listed the things in the order that she knew was right for her, giving each item a different color:

Prayer and church attendance	blue
Les (husband)	red
Children	yellow
Housework	green
Bible study	orange
Prayer group	pink
Counseling others	brown
Friends	maroon
Leisure	heliotrope

Then she made up a daily log to record how she spent each fifteen minutes for an entire week. At the end of the week using different colored marking pens she colored in each square. The time spent in prayer was blue, time with and for her husband Les was red and so on. What she discovered was amazing. She had lots of blue, orange, pink, quite a bit of brown and green, hardly any red or yellow and only a thin line of maroon and heliotrope. (Another woman might discover lots of red and yellow and almost no blue, orange or green, showing imbalance in another direction.)

Using the time-management principles of purpose, goals, priorities and plans Evelyn was able to keep her purpose which she knew was right and reevaluate her goals, priorities and plans. She said she can hardly wait to make another chart when the new plans are in action and see how her new life patterns look in living color.

Each of us who is married is called to channel our gifts into marriage. God has given women great talents and abilities. Our intelligence is equal to men, our stamina and emotional endurance often greater. God does not want us to bury our capabilities but He wants us to use them for the job we've been called to do.

At first glance this looks like it will take us far afield of what we want for ourselves. And yet what do we want? Do we want to have Jesus' life shining through our lives? In the end do we want to be like Christ? Giving up our own plans for our husbands can cause us suffering. Peter, who was crucified upside down for his faith tells us:

> This suffering is all part of the work God has given you. Christ, who suffered for you, is your example. Follow in his steps: He never sinned, never told a lie, never answered back when insulted; when he suffered he did not threaten to get even; he left his case in the hands of God who always judges fairly (1 Peter 2:21-23 TLB).

How will putting the plans, the desires and dreams of a husband before our own give us more, even enough time?

Actually, it sounds like biting off more than we can chew and getting further behind than we already are. But time will be ours in greater abundance for at least two reasons. First, a happy unthreatened husband who knows he is the head of our house and first in our lives is easy to live with. One of the great thieves of our time is a lack of energy, for time has no value if we cannot use it. Unlike money it cannot be saved for another day. An upset household, a not-going-too-well household and especially an unhappy household robs us of our energy and steals our time. We all know the woman who is so irritated with herself, her husband or her neighbor that she seems to accomplish little else. This is because her energy has gone into her irritation, making her time valueless.

Second, God gives the time to us to accomplish what He wants us to do in our lives, even in each hour of the day. *Purpose, goals, priorities and plans are useful tools only as our lives are in right order.* When we are doing what God wants us to do, I'm not sure how it happens but I know it is true, He, who is the giver of time, gives us the time to do it.

So, we who are married, can add another row of the deeply colored aqua beneath the sailing ship. Supported by prayer first and our marriage in its rightful place, the beautiful clipper will sail ahead on her course in safe waters.

6
The Miserable Years

Many years ago there was a story in the *Woman's Home Companion* of a young woman who, like myself at the time, had four little children underfoot at once. Her immediate problem was to get the house ready, the children cleaned, and dinner fixed before the arrival of her mother-in-law, who had always been the ideal mother. Everything went wrong, of course.

To complicate her troubles, well-meaning friends dropped in and insisted that she should slow down. They said the very things she knew her mother-in-law would also say, "These are the happy years; just enjoy them." My magazine friend, coping with a basket of sand in the middle of the kitchen floor still wet with wax, two formerly spotless toddlers who had managed to find a mud puddle and a baby who had pulled the nipple off her bottle and dumped eight ounces of soybean milk into the davenport could only sigh and dutifully repeat with the same spirit, "These are the happy years. I know they must be the happy years."

With everything at its worst she looked out the window to see her mother-in-law coming up the walk. As she opened the door, she began to apologize and excuse the mess and, trying to make her husband's mother like her she said, "Now I don't mind a bit about all this mess. I know that these are the happy years."

The older woman sat down, held up her hand and ex-claimed, "My dear, these are not the happy years; these are the miserable ones. Your job at this point is just to live through them." The young mother burst into tears and then into laughter and declared her mother-in-law the most un-derstanding woman she had ever known.

Now this might be a little strong for some mothers to take. But for every wonderful Christian mother I have met who tells me how glorious life is with several children underfoot, I've met a dozen other wonderful Christian mothers who say, "These kids are driving me crazy. What am I going to do?"

To put it in a little softer way, I read of a man who said:

> I was on an airplane heading towards Chicago when the stewardess announced that we were coming into some turbulence and should fasten our seat belts. Sure enough, the plane rocked and pitched and bumped along until some of the passengers were ill. Then, as suddenly as it had started, the turbulence stopped and the ride became smooth and we sailed easily into our landing.

> So it is with children. It is almost inevitable to encounter turbulence, even some nauseating turbulence, in the rearing of a family. Our job is not to like it but to see it through, knowing that there is a smooth landing on the other side.

I can say from experience that no matter how miserable the miserable years might be, how terrible it becomes through the years of the teen-ager, no matter how "rotten" our own children may appear in comparison to someone else's , that if we will stick in there, keep our rules, keep on being the mothers that we know we have been called to be, there is a safe landing on the other side. Children *do* grow up and when they get older, sometimes just a little older, we find they have not at all departed from the ways that we have taught them (cp. Proverbs 22:6).

The books on child rearing are numerous. Some have the religious approach, others, the secular approach, the social approach or the psychological approach. This isn't a book that is going to give any more conflicting advice to what must be the most advised generation of parents ever. During a time when I had read all the articles that analyzed and advised (and was trying in vain to take all the advice) a friend brought a magazine home from the store with a lead article entitled, "The Seven Deadly Wrongs Each Parent Commits Daily." It was too much. My friend looked at me and I at her. Then we burst out laughing. "I promise not to read it if you don't," she said.

Since the subject here is how does a Christian mother find enough time, I'm not going to advise you or attempt to analyze any mother's seven deadly wrongs. Instead, I'd like to present one basic self-evident fact about children that, like the trees in a forest, was too close for me to see for some time. However, when I saw it in all its implications, I somehow sensed I had left the miserable years behind. Not the turbulence, that's always there, but much of the worry that was stealing hunks of my time. The basic fact is this: *children take time.*

Therein lies the misery. There is so much we want to do, so much needing to be done in this world of ours, so much that society insists that we must do. We must not have ring-around-the-collar, we must have floors that gleam until we can see our faces in them, we must have furniture that reflects an arranged bouquet in living color. We must cook gourmet meals, be publicly aware, socially active, academically current. Then, of course, we have the children to take care of and the children take so much time.

> It takes half an hour to feed a toddler breakfast.
>
> Half an hour to bathe and dress him.
>
> Half an hour to clean up what he shouldn't

have gotten into.

It takes half an hour to sit with a four-year-old working a puzzle for the first time.

It takes half an hour to listen to a six-year-old's reading lesson.

It takes half an hour to coach a teen-ager in history.

It takes twenty minutes to share a cup of camomile tea with a young daughter.

It takes uncountable hours to drive a car pool.

It takes fifteen minutes, six times a day to discipline a child who has decided to test you.

It takes fifteen minutes each night to listen to each child's prayers.

The very fact that we have a child in our care, our own or someone else's, means that we have been called by God to be a parent to that child. In the divine order, we have been seeking the kingdom of God first, loving and revering and giving our time to our husbands second. The loving care we give our children is the third most important thing we can do with our time. Certainly we must do as the Bible says and train up a child in the way that he should go so that when he is older he will not depart from it (cp. Prov. 22:6). But training up a child takes time. We are also told not to provoke our children to anger but discipline them and instruct them in the Lord (cp. Col. 3:21). Unfortunately, discipline takes both time and energy, and instruction in the Lord must go on and on.

As we add training, disciplining and instructing to the list of feeding, cleaning, teaching, listening and supporting, it's easy to see why we may be miserable. All these things that must be done with our children are at war with all that society tells us or that we tell ourselves we must do elsewhere.

For me the war ended abruptly and with it, the misery, with the realization that I didn't have to be any of those people that magazines so subtly insisted I should be. I didn't have to be a great housekeeper or an enviable cook. I didn't have to wear any of those "hats" that the good people at our church thought everyone should wear, that of teacher, organizer, committee member. I didn't have to be any of the women that the school and the media insisted were so important: the politically involved, the champion of the downtrodden or even the exciting, innovative hostess.

Sometimes we make life so complicated and get our time so parceled out that half an hour for a child's story or two hours for an afternoon game or fifteen minutes to clean up a quart of spilled milk throws our schedule and our dispositions into a fury. Dr. James Dobson observes:

> It is obvious that many families live on this kind of last minute, emergency schedule, making it impossible to meet the demands of their own over-commitments. Why do they do it? The women whom I surveyed admitted their dislike for the pace they kept, yet it has become a monster which defies containment. Faster and faster they run, jamming more and more activities into their hectic days. Even their recreation is marked by the same breakneck pace.[1]

There seems a parallel between this busyness that tempts us away from our children and the subtle temptation the devil used to test Jesus in the wilderness. As Satan attempted to turn Jesus from His course by quoting Scripture he also tries to subtly detour us by suggesting something quite good for us to do. There's only one problem—that good thing isn't what God has called us to. Jesus answered Satan with more Scripture and we can do the same. When we are tempted away from being the parents God has called us to be we can quote, " . . . Anyone who lets himself be distracted from the work I plan for him is not fit for the Kingdom of God" (Luke 9:62 TLB).

If we have been called by God to be mothers, let's drop all the activities that are making it so painful for us to enjoy our children. For everyone says, "But society needs me. I can't sit back and not do my share." I would say, *"Let's give our children the time they need to help them grow into secure people."* We are adding a greater burden to society than we could ever compensate for with all our good deeds if we don't spend time training our children or if we don't spend time helping them to be secure as people.

Geri Rochon, mother-in-law to Dave, one of our older sons, is a woman who trained her children well. She took the time to teach them and, even better, she took the time to call them back over and over again, if necessary, to do the job right. Her daughter, Annette, Dave's wife, is a responsible young woman who isn't harried at all by the demands of marriage. The time her mother spent is reaping a reward in a daughter who is able to take her rightful place in society as a wife and mother.

For those who would say, "But I can't stop what I'm doing at church. I'm doing the Lord's work," I would say to them, *"Taking care of our children* is *the Lord's work* and if we don't spend time training our children in the ways of the Lord, then helping out at church is a mockery."

One of my Alaskan pen pals, Carol Chittenden, said that the Lord had spoken to her heart about the time she was spending in church-related activities. "He said He did not want me to use the time that belongs to my family for what I might think is His work. My family has a right to a proportion of my time and this right of theirs has a high priority in God's view."

My friend Judy, the mother of three little blonds and a black-haired Korean child, prayed and prayed for God to show her the great task He had for her to do for Him. Certainly, it was something earthshaking, she thought as she prayed all winter. Then slowly, slowly as the days turned into spring, it became clear to her that God *did* have something great for her to do and she was already doing it. The day-by-day constant caring for her children was indeed accomplishing something great in the kingdom of God.

After we moved to our new house, our local parish church urged all the adults to come to a special meeting. Two people had called and said, "I hope you're coming." I had agreed that it sounded interesting. But that night Katy, then nine years old, said, "Mama, when are you going to teach me the twenty-third Psalm like you promised?" The experience I'd had of being "too busy" when her older brother and sister were young had taught me that there was no meeting at church as important as one little nine-year-old girl. I sat beside her bed, as my mother had sat beside mine many times, and began the age-old shepherd's prayer. "The Lord is my shepherd; I shall not want" (Psa. 23:1). She repeated the words back and we went over and over it until finally it was locked into her memory.

Two days later just as I was about to return home from a trip to town the car had a flat tire. I limped to a gas station grateful that one was so close. But the attendants couldn't change the tire as long as there were customers. As it grew dusky, I grew concerned over Katy. In the winter, dark comes quickly and this was her guitar lesson day. I knew she was standing in front of the school waiting for me all alone in what was still a strange neighborhood. There was no way to reach her and I felt fear for her. Finally I called Bill at work and asked him to go. When he reached the school, Katy was waiting all alone, huddled next to her guitar on one of the school's steps.

That evening I sat beside her bed. "Honey, what did you think of while you sat there on those steps? Were you afraid?"

She smiled. "At first I was. Then I started the twenty-third Psalm and I just kept saying over and over, 'Yea, though I walk through the valley of the shadow of death, I will fear no evil: for thou art with me . . . ' (Psa. 23:4). The more I said it, the more I wasn't afraid."

Many, many times older women have said to me, "If I had
my life to live over, I would give more time to my children." A
great Christian leader recently wrote, "If I could begin again I
would spend more time with my family doing 'non-Christian'
things."

Giving time to our children also gives a gift to the next
generation. If bad experiences produce bad effects for five
generations as some psychologists claim, then good experiences must do the same. I remember the day we built the
snowmen. Bill Jr., Dave and Mary Therese were all little and
Anne was the baby. Snow had unexpectedly fallen and the
children were clamoring to go out in it. As I bundled them into boots and snow pants and related paraphernalia, our
neighbor Lois, who was probably ten years older than I, appeared at the front door pulling her Mary and Joanie on a
sled. "Pat, come out and play in the snow."

"Me? I don't have the time."

"Come on. You can spare the time."

"No, besides I'm too old to play in the snow."

"You'll look back and regret it if you don't."

Reluctantly I bundled myself and the baby and out we
went while I tried not to think of the oatmeal drying on the
dishes still on the table. The children laughed with one
another and created comical carrot and coal faces on
their assorted snowmen. By lunch time we stood back and
proudly admired our lumpy creations that grinned their
frozen smiles at us.

"They look like Mom when she's gonna have a baby," one
of them said.

Bill Jr. stepped close to me. "It wouldn't have been so
much fun if you hadn't come, too."

Today each of them is gone, each with their own lives and
some even with babies. Lois was so right. I would have regretted missing that day far more than I ever regretted not
scraping the oatmeal off the breakfast dishes. Although I'm
sure the children have forgotten that morning, perhaps it still
remains in their subconscious. Someday perhaps it will be the

most natural thing in the world for them to take their young children out in the snow and build a family of snow people that look just like a pregnant mom.

This morning two-year-old Patrick said, "Mom, I want to hold your hand at the beach." No one had to say, "Come on you'll regret it if you don't go," for I had learned. We went, the two of us, and overturned rocks, awakened sleepy crabs, peeked into tide pools and fed bread to the gulls. Once again the work waited and once again I would have regretted missing that special time.

Whenever we give, it seems we receive more. One of the greatest bonuses of giving time to our children is a peaceful household. Even when we have made terrible mistakes in the past with our kids, a new beginning to be the mother we have been called by God to be will bring about a new peace in our house and in our family.

If we have made these the miserable years by trying to cram too much into too little available time, then let's back up and cut out the extras so we can build a happy life-style for our families.

As for the picture puzzle, let's set another line of aquamarine pieces of supportive water beneath the beautiful clipper. Seeking the Father, loving our husbands, letting our children have our time gives us an even deeper flowing channel through which we can sail confidently as we journey on.

7

To Meet
or
Not To Meet

When I think of the early years of my married life and remember the house on Twelfth Avenue and our tiny old church on the side of a hill, I recall with a dose of nostalgia, an unlikely collection of women known as St. Mary's Circle, a group of ladies living within seven square blocks of the church. It seems dull in explaining it — I even believe we looked dull and probably we sounded dull. But the truth is, we weren't at all. We met once a month and I counted the days until each meeting. There was Millie, who always brought her Aunt Nora; the three sisters Betty, Mary and Jeanette, who seemed to enjoy each other best. There was old Mrs. Balliau and old Mrs. Moschetto with her half a dozen or so teeth. There were the good cooks, Charlotte and Inez, and Lois and Doris who laughed a lot.

Of all of them I was the most unlikely member. I was eighteen, by far the youngest, and the only one who brought a baby. I went because Bill was at night school where he spent most evenings. We had no money and I was lonely. Those wonderful women loved me and Bill Jr. and welcomed us into their circle meeting. Old Mrs. Balliau sympathized with the difficulties of a baby. She remembered her days of child rearing with descriptions of a backyard washing tub and old

Mrs. Moschetto shared her philosophy of a successful marriage: "More spaghetti, feed him more spaghetti and everything will be fine!" To me it was like a Tupperware party where I didn't have to buy anything or a baby shower where I didn't have to scrimp on the groceries to bring a gift. I remember the night they elected me secretary. They made it seem so important and I came home proud to tell Bill the happy news. He had come home from school and fallen asleep. "Bill, Bill, guess what? I'm the secretary of St. Mary's Circle!"

He couldn't comprehend its importance. "What's so good about that?"

"They elected me."

Still it was lost on him. He saw, I suppose, just a group of ordinary ladies instead of friends who had become so important to me. Undaunted by Bill's lack of interest, I may well have been the most enthusiastic secretary St. Mary's Circle ever had.

I continued to look forward to attending those meetings until after our fourth child was born and someone higher up in the parish decided the circle should be phased into something more meaningful. So St. Mary's Circle disbanded but even now, when chance permits me to run into one of those dear older ladies or perhaps one of the three sisters, we stop for a moment in the aisle of the supermarket or in the vestibule after a funeral and remember a time when going to a meeting was so much fun.

Never once did I stop and wonder if St. Mary's Circle was God's will for me. If anyone had asked, I probably would have given him a blank stare and mumbled, "Er . . . well, why shouldn't it be?" But looking back now I can say, "Certainly it was." Applying Dr. Engstrom's measuring sticks of purpose, goals, priorities and planning, I can see that my *purpose* was to receive and give friendship. The *goal* was this once-a-month meeting and whatever work it entailed. Its *priority* in my life made sense. It was more important than a shopping trip but not nearly as important as an ailing child. The *plan-*

ning was a matter of saving the first Tuesday and finding the seventy-five cents to pay the baby-sitter after there were too many children to bring.

There came a time, inevitably I guess, when Bill was through with school, and Johnny was ill, when meeting piled upon meeting, good work upon good work, time away from home upon time away from home. Religious education, the Food Bank, money raising. Often it wasn't fun but grim and necessary as work had to be done and there were so few willing to give themselves to do it. I was leaving the family more and more as I concerned myself with those things that we do as Christians.

If I had known then about purpose and goals it might have made a big difference. At that time I had not even heard of priorities in daily living. My purpose for all this activity was no longer friendship but more a desire to be a concerned Christian. A concerned Christian usually taught or was a student of religious education and was concerned with community and political needs. There was not even a semi-worthwhile request I could say no to. Many times I left the children to their own devices so I could do something "worthwhile" such as visit the hospital, ring doorbells for a school levy or prepare clothing for the needy.

As I look back, I believe the worst part of all was my own self-righteousness. Mother called one day and in her lovely way tried to be tactful about what she saw as an obvious want. "Dear, I called earlier but Bill Jr. said you were helping a neighbor."

"Oh, yes, poor thing. She certainly needs my help."

"What do the children do while you are gone?"

"Oh, they play be themselves."

Mustering up her courage she replied, "Maybe you should stay home with them instead."

I was indignant. "Don't you know Jesus said a cup of cold water given in His name is done unto Him?"

Still vivid is the day that Mother's unspoken thoughts became graphic. I was asked to be part of an inner-city team to put on a gigantic theatrical production. Its purpose was to keep kids off the streets in the summer. The first brainstorming session was exhilarating. Certainly we were getting down to the nitty gritty of Christian response by offering something that directly affected people's lives. I dashed home at lunch to see how the family was getting along. As I pulled up in front of the house a police car pulled up behind me. In the backseat sat two frightened eight and nine-year-old boys. I stopped and stared, hardly believing my eyes. The policeman turned to me, "Are these your boys, Ma'am?"

I gulped, "Yes."

It turned out that, with a third boy named Jeff, they had climbed through the window of Jeff's locked house, stolen some matches and had hidden in the brush of a vacant lot to light forbidden firecrackers. The lot had caught fire and the boys were apprehended by the neighbors. I took them into the house, called the inner-city office and reported I wouldn't be able to help with the production after all. It was suddenly obvious which kids I should be keeping off the streets that summer.

It was at this point I began to do some needed evaluating in my life and time. No longer was I enjoying the simple outreach of the circle meeting. Instead my life was being run and ruined by a host of activities I could not or would not say no to.

Denise Adler, the Bible teacher, speaking from the experience she's had with scores of women whom she meets in her classes comments:

> I constantly say, "Slow me down, Lord." I have a strong drive in me to get in there and get it done and when I'm running at a fast pace and doing, doing, I get ahead of the Lord. Too many of us do this and we begin to tackle jobs the Holy Spirit didn't mean for us to do. We start all fired up and instead of asking the Lord what He wants to bless, we ask Him to bless what we've started. When He doesn't we fizzle out.
>
> In particular this is one of the greatest problems of

Christian women and the reason why they fret over their Christian work and the reason they do not feel fulfilled. We all know the Bettys and Lindas who take on a job with eagerness and then begin to do it less eagerly and then poorly until they have to be reminded to do it at all. They aren't happy or eager anymore. They feel badly about themselves and pretty soon personality problems develop. They leave the job and possibly the church. None of this would have had to happen if they had prayed first and made sure the Holy Spirit wanted this activity for them. Even worse, the Bettys and Lindas who move ahead of the Lord usually become restless, unhappy women in other areas of their lives because when one area gets out of whack, it affects everything.

I would say to the Christian woman who is feeling unfulfilled that she should take a good hard look at her activities and see where she has taken on a responsibility that isn't for her. It could even be that a perfect job for her situation and talent is going undone while she struggles at something that isn't what the Holy Spirit intended for her. In addition, when any of us undertakes a work that is not meant for us, we deprive the person whom it was meant for in the first place.

My own great regret is that I have not seen that the Scripture about a "cup of cold water given in my name" applied directly to my family (Matt. 10:42). I wonder how I could have been so concerned for the world at large and so unconcerned for the tiny world God had given me specific care of. Here were the naked to clothe, the sick to care for and the hungry to feed. Here were wounds to bind, the cup of cold water to be continually given in Jesus' name. But I began to learn that following Christ doesn't necessarily mean doing what looks right or what other people think is right. Instead, it means discerning in my heart what I've been called to do and saying no to what I haven't been called to.

As I look back over the years I have found five interests beyond my family that I do not regret. These five things I did over a period of twenty-five years. Just as the Proverbs 31 lady who rose up in the morning and did so many wonderful things, we must remember she did not do them all in one day but over a period of a lifetime. So, too, these five things that I do not regret extend over all of my married years. One is the hours and hours of college night classes I took after Bill finally obtained his degree. Evaluating that now, I would say my purpose was the need of mental stimulation that a household filled with little children failed to provide. The goal was the class itself. The priority was that it was never more important than the family. The planning included classes in the evening when I was least needed at home.

I have no regrets about time spent in children's religious classes. The purpose was to share in the educational processes of our church. The goals, priorities and planning made sense.

I have no regrets about Cheri. Cheri was a young unwed mother (named, she said, for someone in a Frankie Laine song) who spent hours and hours with our family often sharing some of the misery of her background. I remember how pregnant and alone she was, so broke that all she had to wear on her feet were a pair of men's maroon argyle socks with high-heeled sandals.

After the baby was born Cheri could hardly put up with it alone. She would often come and sit in our noisy household just to be with another adult. As time healed her wounds we eventually saw less and less of her. Today she is working among disadvantaged people and loving it. Purpose — giving friendship. Goals — welcoming her when she came. Priorities — this is hard to answer. Cheri did take my time from the children and yet I wonder if she didn't bring them something in its place. Mary Therese, my older daughter, had been a youngster then but one time after she was married and up in the middle of the night feeding her new baby, she heard a cry outside. She went to the window and saw the ending of a neighborhood fracas. Police cars and an ambulance started zooming up her street. The man from across the way was taken away in a police car; his wife, severely beaten, in an ambulance. Mary Therese wrapped her baby in a blanket and dashed outside. "Don't worry about your children," she told the young woman in the ambulance, "I'll stay with them until you can come home."

The next day I asked her, "How did you have the courage to rush up to a woman you didn't know?"

She replied thoughtfully, "I don't know. I just thought of Cheri and knew that I should go."

Planning—how would anyone plan filling a need like this? Maybe in regard to people it's good to plan to be flexible. (There is a point where people can take too much time and this should be a matter of discernment. For their own good they should not be allowed to do it. Sometimes I said to Cheri "It's time for you to go home. I'm weary.")

The fourth item I have no regret over was the taking of an avocation. For me, it was writing. For others it may be art, cake decorating, sewing, cooking or countless other things. Here is where the four checks are important. An honest look at purpose, goals, priorities and planning should make an avocation a joy instead of a regret.

The fifth on my list is Barbie. Barbie was fourteen months old when she came to live with us, nearly three years old when she left us to be adopted. In between those two dates I lived the most hectic time of my life. Barbie's I.Q. was in the genius level and her outlandish curiosity would overrule any thoughts she might have had about obedience. There was no place she couldn't climb, investigate and disrupt. On a typical day, she made steps out of a chest of drawers, and using them as a ladder reached up to the shelf and pulled a combination of a Monopoly game, a Scrabble game, several picture puzzles and Chinese Checkers off onto the floor. While I was cleaning them up I heard a drip, drip, drip and found water was pouring into the kitchen from the ceiling. I ran upstairs to discover Barbie had flooded the upstairs bathroom once again.

There is no doubt that Barbie took time, a great deal of time from the family. Mother voiced her concern. She had grown quite forthright by then. "Now, I'm not worried about Katy: she and Barbie are so close in age that what you do for one you do for the other but it's Joe I'm concerned with. It's hard on him having that active little girl around taking the time that rightfully belongs to him."

But when Barbie left and I sat down in the big chair to weep over her going, it was five-year-old Joe who climbed into my lap to weep with me. "Mama, Mama, why did she have to go? I loved her so much. She was my sister."

We have been called to follow Christ. *We seek Him first. We are wives next, if that is our calling, mothers after that.* We are daughters and daughters-in-law and often mothers-in-law. There are times when we do nothing outside our homes and other times when we reach out to our community when we are confident we are not doing the job someone else was supposed to do and confident we are doing only what God has called us to.

As we apply the purpose, goals, priorities and plans to this area of our lives we can fill in more of the blue and white background. Behind us now the sky is growing in color and looking favorable for sailing. Beneath us we can fit together more of the deep aquamarine. For when this fourth part of our lives is in order, there is great depth to the water that supports the beautiful clipper.

8
Getting to Know Me

Brother Andrew, the famed missionary of *God's Smuggler,*[1] tells a story of a woman who lived in the same Christian boarding house as he did who always missed the tram in the morning. After the tenth time she mentioned at breakfast while dawdling, "I wonder what the Lord is trying to say to me by the number of times I have missed this tram?"

"Well, Sister," Brother Andrew said, "it seems very simple to me. He's telling you to get going earlier."

When I heard this story it seemed as though the Lord was saying to me, "There, do you see how important it is to know yourself?" Even a little self-knowledge can make a big difference in the way a day is spent. I could see our boarding-house friend sitting there at a broad oak table crammed into a stiff but proper dining room. She licked the last crumb of muffin and marmalade from her finger tips, downed the last drop of strong breakfast tea. She should be going; in fact, she mentions it to the two retired boarders across the table. And yet she sits just another minute longer. Again she announces, "I must be going." And again, she dawdles.

Then in a last-minute flurry, she pushes the chair back, grabs her coat and topples the coat-tree, calls for assistance in finding her umbrella (somebody moved it) and with hat askew she runs out the door to the great relief of everyone. As usual the tram goes by before she gets to the corner and the second tram brings her to her job, clamoring up the stairs, panting and into her place a few minutes late. We can hear her announcing breathlessly to her co-workers, "You have no idea what I must go through each morning to get out of that boarding house."

Truly, all the inconvenience to herself and others is simply a matter of not knowing herself and where she could go for help. I believe a gentle word to the Lord during her morning devotions would have been enough. "Dear Lord, You know I'm such a slow starter on my own. Will You help me leave the table as soon as tea is finished?" Just that modicum of self-knowledge and prayer would have allowed her to find her coat and pin her hat in place, locate her umbrella and walk to the tram in a genteel way. She could have been in her place, at nine o'clock, instead of dashing through the streets like a reckless delivery boy and causing interruption for her co-workers.

Brother Andrew may have been right; the Lord was telling her to leave earlier, but through her He is telling us something far more important. He is telling us that we use our time to its greatest advantage when we have learned to know ourselves.

We have the example of Jesus who knew Himself better than anyone else. He stated without hesitation, "I am the way, the truth and the life . . . " (John 14:6 TLB). There was no vacillating, no wavering as to His purpose. He walked with His disciples after the Last Supper on His way to Gethsemane and explicitly told them what His wife was all about. " . . . No man cometh unto the Father except by me" (John 14:6 TLB). When He had ascended into heaven, His disciples no doubt stayed up all night, many nights, talking, talking, talking. Their hands made gestures, their voices grew loud as each remembered something new. Everything He did had purpose. He knew so well why the Father had sent Him. He seemed to have a deep knowledge of Himself. He also knew when He needed to be alone to pray and when He needed to be alone with them. He had a mission and He knew what that mission was. He knew Himself.

I wonder, do we know ourselves? We know we've been called to follow Jesus but do we know this person who's been called to follow Him and be a woman in today's world? We have to know what she is like and how she goes about doing things. We have to know ourselves. Let's start by finding out about our temperament. I believe the alignment of temperament traits stems from four basic types.

While psychologists have given these temperament types classical names, I have dubbed them with names we women can identify more easily with. There are:

—the *slow-to-get moving* type
—the *get-in-and-tackle-it-now* personality
—the *I-could-care-less* creative person
—the *we'll-do-it-this-way-immediately* woman.

While the Holy Spirit changes our lives when He touches us, energizing the slower woman and slowing down the too-busy woman, I believe we still must live with our basic, often inherited temperaments.

Knowing this is an aid to knowing ourselves. It's important that we know the kind of person we are so that we can know the kind of response we should make to the ideas in this book. We are all so different that every idea could not possibly apply to every one of us. We have to look them all over and try them on to see which become us.

The *get-in-and-tackle-it-now* person shouldn't feel about an idea, "For heaven's sake, everyone does that anyway." The *slow-to-get-moving* type shouldn't think, "Oh, my, I can't do all this at once." Each should take what is right for her temperament and her purpose and goals and apply only that to her situation. *At no time should a suggestion ever make us feel condemned.*

I remember two mothers in a discussion group I attended. Each admired the other and secretly determined she would pattern her life after her friend. *Slow-to-get-moving* Helen was a wonderful wife and mother but a terrible housekeeper. She would drop her work in a minute to go fishing with her husband or play house or Monopoly with her children. *Get-in-and-tackle-it-now* Ginger was the opposite. Her housework came first and, only when it was done and everything sparkled, could she stop and go with her husband or force herself to join a game of Clue. It was easy to see why the two admired each other. Helen saw Ginger's perpetually shining house and decided, "I'm not going to do one thing with this family until the house is clean each day." Ginger observed Helen's easygoing way with her family and her family's relaxing response to life and declared in her heart, "I don't care how rotten this house looks. I'm going to spend time with the children every day before I clean it."

Helen lasted the longer, sticking it out for five weeks. During that time the house had never been so clean nor easygoing Helen so crabby. Although her family had praised her efforts in the beginning, they finally begged her to quit following Ginger's routine and be her own sweet self. Helen complied, yet she still longed for a nice neat house.

Ginger lasted four days. Playing Scrabble while the laundry molded (she was certain it was going to) or running off to look at a piece of real estate with her husband and coming home to dishes in the sink was too contrary to her temperament. In one evening, a furious rampage, brought on by the disorder around her, wiped out, at least in Ginger's mind, all the goodwill she had built up in four days of "enjoying" the children.

Back in the discussion group each confided her failure. Enough time had passed so each woman could laugh at herself but the discussion leader, aware of each personality and sensing each woman's desire to change for the better, offered her viewpoint. "Helen, I know you want to keep a better house. Ginger, I know you sincerely want to spend more time with your family. Both of you are trying to change on your own power. Let the Holy Spirit be your power. Instead of trying to be each other, why don't you seek to be the person you know Jesus has called you to be?''

Helen agreed to pray for the grace to spend an hour a day on her housework. Ginger agreed to pray for the grace to spend an hour each day doing something interesting with her family. Our group agreed to keep them both in prayer as they tried to be true to their calling and their temperaments.

It worked. As time went on, each learned to live within the framework of her basic temperament and yet changed enough through the Holy Spirit's help to feed confident about her overall role as wife and mother.

This matter of time is so elusive because what one woman regards as valuable use may be a waste to someone else.

The *we-will-do-it-this-way-immediately* woman may be too organized. She may already be getting the most out of every day. Her problem may be riding roughshod over others to find time for her own accomplishment. My friend Andrea, who is a Pacific Northwest artist and has a dozen other projects going as well, tells how she found more time at her easel and other interests by usurping her husband Phil's time. When they had only one car and the children were all little, Phil had done the weekly grocery shopping on his way home from work. Since he prided himself that the only thing he knew how to do in the kitchen was make coffee, he hadn't been tempted by gourmet foods and chance recipes. As a result, he had shopped, if not interestingly, at least economically.

Finally the day came when Andrea had a car of her own and the children were off to school. Andrea began to do the grocery shopping and she discovered what a job she had been saved from all those years. It took all day, it seemed, and, what's more it was ruining her schedule. After a few months she decided that, since Phil could do it better and easier, why not ask him to continue on with the job? She confided it was a relief to have that day back again.

Of course, when Phil shopped on the way home from work, it added another hour and a half to his already long day. Dinner was later; the one who did the dishes was in the kitchen later and the evening confusion, with groceries stacked on the floor beside the refrigerator as well as all over the counter, was far greater than normal.

Andrea knew before too many shopping days went by that she was wrong to impose this situation on everyone in the family so that she could have an extra day. She hated to give up the time it was saving for her personally. If she had been earning the family's living, the story might have had a different ending. As it was, there was no great turning point. As a Christian she knew selfishness was wrong and when the still small voice of the Holy Spirit within her grew loud enough, she said to Phil, "What I'm doing with my time isn't worth this confusion. I think I'll start shopping again."

He gave her statement wholehearted approval. Knowing this about herself now—that she uses other people's time to find time for herself—has made Andrea far more interested in finding time-savers that will help her without taking time from others.

Jeannie is another *get-in-and-tackle-it-now* personality who appears to others to have everything under control. Because housework came easily to her, her house was always clean and there was time for coffee with her friends, everyone thought Jeannie was well-organized. But despite the way it looked, Jeannie knew she wasn't getting the most out of her day. She had much she wanted to do and she sensed there was time to do it. But where? Just knowing, that despite what others said, she wasn't doing her best gave her a new willingness to explore ways to find time. She did discover the time she needed for that something extra. Today her contemporary sketches are in great demand.

Sandra, another type of the *slow-to-get-moving* woman, my neighbor, was more than happy to drop whatever she was doing, to put on a pot of coffee and chat with a friend. She was wonderfully casual until something rather earthshaking happened to her. Sandy met the Holy Spirit and found herself with a new lease on life. All those years of listening to people and caring about them had prepared her to be a favorite group study leader. But Sandy, who had never cared a lick for housework, had to put her house in order weekly so the group could come to her home. We discussed the planning and schedules that are in the next chapter. Sandy, who knew herself well enough to know she was never going to be Mrs. Clean, put the schedules to use as they best fit her. Her whole family rejoiced with her at what planning could do.

My friend Betty, the *I-could-care-less* creative type, drove both me and herself crazy. Her dishes, washing, and sewing could all be piled around the kitchen while Betty sat serenely at the table sewing two thousand sequins on a tap dance outfit. And this is the part that got me; she enjoyed it. The part that got to Betty was her husband who wanted dinner and a clean shirt.

Betty just could not motivate herself into a routine. "I really don't care about the housework: I'll do it later," she said. And yet, she really longed to keep up with the work and also do the detailed sewing that she liked so much. But Betty knew that change was needed in her life. "I just don't want to change," she confided, "but I'm going to ask Jesus to make me *want* to change." In time she did change. Using her time well paid off the biggest dividends for Betty, in terms of her marriage and her self-image, of anyone I have known. She told a group of leaders recently, "It was hard to do all that planning. But I knew it had to be done or I would always be dissatisfied with myself."

So there are all kinds of problems to meet in getting the most out of our time or, as some say, getting the most time out of the day, and all kinds of temperaments to work with. Knowing ourselves and admitting our weaknesses before God and asking His help are the first steps.

In addition to knowing ourselves, *we must know our situation* and not expect to put more into a day than we have to give. Darlene Zielinski, a young mother who drives one leg of our car pool, is a gal who had unrealistic expectations for herself. "I'm so discouraged," she said one afternoon as I dropped off her children. "I'm not getting anything done."

She had three small children and a new baby. I was about to tell her that for many women in such a situation just getting through the day was enough. Before I could say this, she continued, "I only have one hour a day to do what I want."

"Amazing! Do you actually use it for yourself?"

Indeed she did. She sewed or did spiritual reading on alternate days. She planned ahead what she would read or do before so that she wouldn't waste her hour deciding. She had learned to spend late evening time cutting out material to be sewed in her quiet time. I told her I didn't think she had a problem. She didn't have as much time for everything as she used to have but for someone with a new baby she was doing great.

Her face brightened. She admitted she hadn't stopped to consider her situation. It felt wonderful to know she wasn't doing too badly after all.

Throughout Darlene's life her situation will continually vary. Someday when all four of her children are in school and she has time for herself, spiritual reading and prayer will noticeably change. When all four are teen-agers, she may look nostalgically back to the days when all were little and under her feet and her daughters were not driving around in some strange boy's car.

As time passes and our situation changes we have more or sometimes less time to call our own. Ruth, an older woman, who had more than enough time finds that now she must take care of her elderly mother-in-law and her husband who has had a stroke. Lisa, who seemed to have no time, found some when she came into money enough to hire a maid and, luxury of luxuries, someone to drive the car pool both ways. Merry's three children all left home in a two-month period and changed her life-style completely.

Learning to know ourselves also means *understanding our bodies* and the way our menstrual cycle affects our ability to get work done. When we consider that of all the violent crimes committed by women, 62 percent are committed in the week before their period begins, it tells us that our hormones are certainly to be taken into consideration.

Very few women can say that they are the same, month in and month out without any ups and downs. Just before our menstrual periods many of us gain weight, swell up here and there, feel heavy and uncomfortable and often find that we are crabbier than we would like to admit. Being a Christian woman who sincerely loves the Lord does not make us immune to what doctors call premenstrual tension.

A woman whose mind is on the Lord will probably not dwell on herself as she used to, but she does know that there are a few days each month when added burdens make everything else far more difficult than they ordinarily would. This is not the time to begin a new project or embark on a new work-planning program. Dr. William Nolen writes, "If you will concede, as I will, that the most miserable person in the world is the woman in the grip of a severe attack of premenstrual tension, then you will also have to concede that the second most miserable person is whoever is closest to her."[2] If we take Dr. Nolen at his word and consider that our family will no doubt be as miserable as we are, we can plan for their sakes and ours as well. The time before our period may be the time to put at the top of our list, "Put feet up today, read, listen to tapes and enjoy the misery."

As each woman reads this book it will help if she keeps in mind her temperament and her life-style. Why not take a moment now to ask yourselves, "What is my temperament? What are my needs? What do I want to accomplish?" Then let us pray together that the Holy Spirit will guide and convict our hearts where an idea for more time is right for us and keep us from condemnation when an idea isn't for us. Then let's ask Him to keep us constantly filled with His strength to make whatever changes we need to find enough time.

9

Make it a Game

Before we can set sail, before we can even expect the winds of the Holy Spirit to set us on our course as Christian homemakers, we have to make some plans. But so often just the thought of planning sounds terrible, as if the rest of our lives we are going to have to spend dreary hours being a dull planning committee of one if we want to get our work done. A line from my childhood remembrances has given me a different outlook. My mother always said of planning, "Why not make it a game?"

As girls, my sister Wanda and I balked over much of the work expected of us. The job we hated most was washing the windows on the French doors. French doors are always double and ours had fifteen glass panes in each one. Counting both sides of both doors, it added up to sixty little windows. Our house had three sets of these horrible glass rectangles or 180 little windows to be washed several Saturdays a year *before* we could think of going to the Saturday afternoon movie. Each one had to be washed with Fels-Naptha soap that dried to a white translucent covering. Then, with soft cloths, this film was wiped away until the window shone.

At Mother's urging we at last learned to make it a game. After covering the windows with the soap and letting it dry, we took a cloth-covered finger and drew a tic-tac-toe design. The loser of the game had to finish up the window, including corners. If the cat got the game, the next loser had to wash all the windows that had been played on. When we made it a game the time flew and the job didn't seem so horrible after all.

As an adult, I've discovered I can make a challenging game out of my work by *planning it backwards.* On a typical Monday morning after the family has departed except for the two youngest, the house looks something like this:

> Dishes from breakfast, lunch making and last night's late evening snacks all over the table and counters.

> The Sunday paper, toys, and always someone's shoes in the living room.

> Scattered paraphernalia, clothing and unmade beds in the bedrooms.

> Wet towels, dirty clothes, empty hangers and candy bar wrappers in the bathroom.

> Dust everywhere.

Faced with a Monday like this we have several choices. One, go back to bed. The trouble with this plan is obvious; the work is still there when we get up and eveything looks worse than it did originally. Two, we can take the kids and walk out on the mess, have a cup of tea with a neighbor or walk around the shopping mall. But this has the same drawbacks as number one. Three, we can sit down at the kitchen table, pour a half cup of coffee, find an old envelope and a pen (or eyebrow pencil or crayon) and make a game of planning backwards.

We should *know our purpose.* Perhaps it is to make living there more enjoyable for the family and ourselves. Perhaps it's the realization that the children need a good example. Perhaps disorder is irritating or embarrassing. For many, becoming the whole persons Christ has called them to be is enough reason. Whatever, it's good to take a minute and find out what the purpose of cleaning up is.

Next, *set a goal*. Let's say the goal this particular Monday morning is order by noon. We begin by writing it at the top of the list. The game is to assign each task a given amount of time as well as a time slot. Just to give an example I'll go through my own Monday morning game plan.

The kitchen is the biggest mess of all—it should take an hour. So, in order to be through at twelve, I must start the kitchen at eleven. The bathroom will take twenty minutes so I should start it at ten-forty. It's going to take fifteen minutes to put away everything in the front room, thirty minutes to vacuum, ten minutes to dust, another twenty minutes to pick up the clothes in the bedroom and fifteen minutes to make three beds. (In my house there are five bedrooms and another two baths and a rec room that I consider the children's work, not mine.) It takes ten minutes to dress myself and twenty minutes to dress my little boy. I spend thirty minutes for prayer and Bible study. So when my coffee cup is empty, the back of the envelope looks like this:

12:00   Order

11:00   Start kitchen

10:40   Start bathroom

10:30   Dust the front room

10:00   Vacuum

 9:45   Start picking up the front room

 9:25   Start picking up bedroom

 9:10   Make beds

 8:50   Dress the children

8:40   Dress myself

8:10   Prayer and study

Of course, this is just my Monday schedule at this particular time. Someone with an infant would have to put in sixty to ninety minutes for feeding the baby (I never used prime
morning time for bathing the baby; it could be done later
when the pace is more leisurely). Someone else might want to
schedule laundry in the morning. In the second chapter, when
I told about a time with my little children, I talked about our
creative time for Johnny each day. That was right for that
time, just as what I'm doing now fits my life today.

The children like the idea of a game. I say to them, "Come
on now, we must have this room done in twenty minutes. Danny, you take these shoes to Paul's room; Patrick, put this
paper in the fireplace. Then hurry back. If we can get it clean
in time then I have a prize in my pocket." So after they hurry
and I hurry we can enjoy our little treat together and then go
on to another project.

Children's help does slow a mother down. It's always
easier to do it ourselves. But from a practical point of view,
the trouble two preschoolers can get into while a mother is
doing something else can undo the best-laid schedule. It's
easier in the long run and generally more satisfying to include
their "help" in the plan.

I also enjoy the challenge of a timed list. It's like playing a
game of Monopoly where the real estate cards are dealt out
and we see how much business can be done in forty-five
minutes. For the perfectionist whose house and life is chaos
because the present job must be done perfectly and nothing
else matters, the timed list is a lifesaver. We have twenty
minutes to clean the bathroom. That means clean the sink
and toilet, hang fresh towels, gather dirty clothes and throw
away the candy bar wrappers. That's all. This is not the day to
recaulk around the tub, scrub the tile or wash the walls.
Twenty minutes is all the time there is. The goal for the day is

order by twelve o'clock noon. It provides us the double discipline, first, to begin the bathroom cleaning, and second, to walk out of the bathroom twenty minutes later.

The great advantage of a list is knowing exactly what has to be done instead of having the irritating feeling that there is so much left to do that I don't know where to begin. One Saturday, Bill and I sat at breakfast and made the usual Saturday chart.

Almost before we were finished the plans changed. The neighbor needed help getting his car started. The kids reported a storm had brought a load of driftwood onto the beach and it had to be gathered before the tide took it out again. Someone picked up some nails in the vacuum cleaner and it had to be taken apart and put back together. So it went. At the end of the day, everything on the list was still undone.

It was two more weeks before we had finished that Saturday's work list. However, neither Bill nor I felt as frustrated as we would have if we had had only a vague feeling of much to be done instead of our chores all written out before us.

Each person will have a different-looking list on the back of her envelope. A neighbor who drives the morning car pool stops at her mother's on the way home each morning for fifteen or twenty minutes. My married daughter, Mary Therese, begins her dinner at nine o'clock each morning because her afternoons are so hectic. Poor health may produce an entirely different game plan. No matter what the schedule, a backward planning list can be used by everyone, including the woman who must get out of the house every morning by seven-thirty with the children.

I can hear people saying, "The list wouldn't work at my house; there are too many interruptions." "I can't be home in the morning." "My husband is always interrupting me." "I'm just not a morning person." Truly as Thoreau once said, "We all march to the beat of a different drummer." But every drummer has his musical score to follow. When that score or list tells what we must do to keep our lives moving, we are able to keep a rhythm to our day instead of experiencing those long, futile pauses that come from looking in vain for our place.

One of the most popular games today is *The $25,000 Game*. Although it sounds like a morning TV show, it actually comes to us from the business world:

> When Charles M. Schwab was president of Bethlehem Steel he confronted Ivy Lee, a management consultant, with an unusual challenge: "Show me a way to get more things done," he demanded. "If it works, I'll pay anything within reason."
>
> Lee handed Schwab a piece of paper. "Write down the things you have to do tomorrow," he said. Schwab did it. "Now number these items in the order of their real importance," Lee continued. Schwab did it. "The first thing tomorrow morning," Lee added, "start working on number one and stay with it until it is completed. Next take number two and don't go any further until it is completed. Then proceed to number three, and so on. If you can't complete everything on schedule, don't worry. At least you will have taken care of the most important things before getting distracted by items of lesser consequence.
>
> "The secret is to do this daily," continued Lee. "Evaluate the relative importance of the things you have to get done . . . establish priorities . . . record your plan of action . . . and stick to it. Do this every working day. After you have convinced yourself of the value of this system, have your men try it. Test it as long as you like. Then send me a check for whatever you think the idea is worth."
>
> In a few weeks Charles Schwab sent Ivy Lee a check for twenty-five thousand dollars. Schwab later said that this lesson was the most profitable one he had ever learned in his business career.[1]

It will work for all of us. Homemakers everywhere are finding great success in applying this to their own household. Here again one of the most important playing tools is *the list*. It is as necessary to *The $25,000 Game* as the Monopoly board is to the Monopoly game. Take an old envelope or file card and begin writing all the tasks that must be done around the house and all the things it would be nice to take time for. A typical list could look like this:

Clean the oven.

Read new Christian book.

Wash hall curtains.

Dust light fixtures.

Write letters.

See if blackberries are ready for picking.

Rearrange rec room.

Wash upstairs windows.

Get clothes ready for Goodwill.

Plant the tulip bulbs in window box.

Make a cake for bake sale.

Obviously, this isn't going to get done in a day or even a week. But the trick to this game is to give each job a priority number. Each woman's list will reflect her household and each woman's priorities will be different. On my list I gave a number ten to the oven. Another woman with an oven like mine might give it a number one. For some women a drive in the country to check the blackberries may be far more important than the upstairs windows. And she can enjoy her outing, knowing there is a plan for the work yet undone.

A third game, and one I like best, is called *Grandma's Game*. It's sort of a combination of the time game and *The*

$25,000 Game. Remember the dishtowels that Grandma used to embroider and were in such neat stacks in the kitchen drawer? Monday - washing, Tuesday - ironing, Wednesday - mending, Thursday - shopping, Friday - cleaning, Saturday - baking, and Sunday - resting. Grandma didn't have our conveniences and she spent all day Monday on the laundry. While I'm grateful that we don't have to wash by hand in water pumped from a well and heated on a wood stove, Grandma's idea of *a special day for a special job* still has merit.

I first started playing the game on the back of an envelope. I listed the days of the week and what I expected myself to do, including attending a Bible study group and grocery shopping. Some gals, in addition to the housework, also have weekly visits to their parents or to rest homes. Some do volunteer work or have a weekly hair or prayer-group appointment. My particular list looks like this:

Monday — The Time Game.

Tuesday — The $25,000 Game.

Wednesday — Bible study.

Thursday — goof off in the morning and grocery shopping in the afternoon.

Friday — The Time Game.

Saturday — laundry and organize the children's work.

Sunday — church and rest.

If goofing off sounds surprising to some, I say, why not? One of the fun parts of being listmakers is setting our own schedule. We often work late in the evening, so why not plan fooling-around-time one morning a week? It's a great help to know that routine isn't all just sticking to something grubby. It may even motivate us when we are tempted to take time off and we know we shouldn't.

In setting plans it helps to know that while we are masters of our day, Jesus is overall Lord of our time. While we can believe that He wants order in our day, He may have another priority for our time on a particular day. There may be somebody we should stop and intercede in prayer for. Perhaps someone needs our counseling and listening. A child may say as mine did last week, "Mommy, I want to hold your hand at the beach." I believe that Jesus, who welcomed the little children, would consider a child's request one of high priority.

In Jesus' life we see how He started off for one place and then, in union with His Father's will, He was stopped by the crowds who needed to be touched by His healing or His teaching or His love.

But I have discovered something wonderful. When we drop our lists and change our plans for His work, an amazing thing happens. Because God is never outdone in generosity He more than makes up for the time we've given. Almost miraculously everything on our lists get done anyway.

There may even be women who are in such union with the Lord that they don't have to make lists. But the rest of us who want to set sail on our grand adventure will begin with the planning that sets our households in order. And as our neighbor who bounced in the back door said, "You know, I'm really enjoying the planning. It's more than a game. Seeing my work get done is an adventure in itself."

10

Barbara's Planner

I had embarrassed her and I was sorry. I'd asked Barbara Shull if she were organized and she'd hemmed and hawed and tried to find the right words but couldn't and I wished I hadn't brought it up. Barbara, dark-haired and pretty, is a wife, mother of three children and the leader of the intercessory prayer group at Aglow, a group that meets weekly and intercedes in prayer for the Aglow fellowships and publications and all the requests that come to the Aglow office by mail.

This type of prayer takes time because Barbara's group prays each need through, sticking with it until they are sure it is answered. And so I had asked, "Barbara, are you an organized person? Do you have the time for this group?"

A friend came to her rescue. "Yes, she's the most organized person I know. She does it all. She manages her cooking, housekeeping, shopping, Little League games, prayer ministry and even little kindnesses for others without feeling or acting rushed."

Barbara's nod said this was true but she was quick to add that she had been searching for the right way to say this because this had not always been so. "Three years ago I couldn't seem to get anything done," she admitted. "Getting dinner on the table was the worst part of all. At four-thirty I'd try to think of a menu and then I'd run to the store and buy something. Then I'd run home and cook it and, of course, dinner was always hurried and always late. Too often when I couldn't face the last-minute planning, we'd go out for another tasteless hamburger. I would look at other women with envy and wonder why they were never as rushed and disorganized as I was. At last I prayed about it: 'Jesus, I'm desperate. I need some help.'

"He told me an amazing thing, 'Make a week's menu.'

"He said that He'd help me," Barbara continued. "Together we worked out what I'd cook for my family for seven nights in a row. He showed me how to make a grocery list from the menu and together we went to the store. For the first time in my married life I went a whole week without agonizing over the evening meal.

"He was so dependable and so practical regarding the dinner problem that I began asking help for every moment of my disorganized life." She smiled at me, "Would you like to see what He did?"

I said I would.

She reached for her purse and took out a notebook she'd put together. "This is the tool that the Lord gave me so I could lead an organized life."

The first page opened out flat and on the left side were spaces for all those items we women never seem to have at our fingertips — social security number, auto license, auto insurance number, etc. Following, there were fifty-two pages, one for each week of the year. On each page was a section for every day of the week.

For each day Barbara had two sections, one called *To Do or Go* and the other labeled *To Write or Call*. There was a third section for menus and a column for a weekly shopping list. She explained, "The *To Do or Go* section is for appointments and errands. I write down all the birthday presents I need to shop for, errands for my husband Fred, the bank, the post office and my friend in a nursing home. It's also for household jobs I wasn't able to find time for before. Now I fit them into days when there is little else scheduled.

"In the *To Call or Write* section I jot down people the Lord brings to my mind to call on, calls for Fred, and any commitments I make for calling others. Also, I put down letters to mail, cards to send and other things I used to put off doing for months at a time. Before I started this I used to constantly go about with the uneasy feeling that there was someone I should contact, but I couldn't remember who."

Barbara explained about the space for her shopping list. As she made out menus to fit her coming weekly schedule (easy ones for busy days) she also wrote down what she'd need at the store to prepare it. "And it's the Lord," she added. "He really cares about us and the little things we have to do. He's the one who showed me all this. With all the remembering written down instead of being a hodgepodge in my mind, He has shown me, too, that I am now free to think of greater things."

There was an advance planning schedule for the coming year where Barbara could write in major commitments. "Easter this year at Dorothy's; optometrist checkback in April; exchange student in February."

The next page was for recipes. "So many times someone has given me a wonderful recipe when I'm at a church dinner or a Little League potluck. I'd think, 'Oh, I'll remember that,' and, of course, I wouldn't. But the Lord showed me that I could add a page to the book to jot these recipes down."

Once more, she talked of the Lord's concern about the little things. "We think He couldn't possibly care about our recipes, but He does. Everything that concerns us concerns Him."

The next two pages were double columns, one side for prayer requests, the other for prayer answers. "So often people have said, 'Will you pray for this?' and then when I took my prayer time either alone or with the intercessory prayer group, I spent important time just trying to remember the requests. Now it's written down and, as the answers come in, I go back and write them down, too. There's nothing quite so faith-lifting as seeing the answers to prayer written out."

The next page over was for birthdays, anniversaries, and gift ideas. Barbara related what we've all experienced in a gift shop. "There I'd be surrounded by hundreds of gift ideas and I couldn't remember what Mother had said she'd really like to have sometime." So next to each special occasion she had jotted down a gift idea she'd heard about or that someone had mentioned they'd like to have.

There was a page for notes. "So many times a speaker would say something so worthwhile I'd write it down and then could never find where I'd written it. Now it's in the book." A note page could be for individual needs, too. Someone on a trip might want to keep track of gas mileage. It's a good place to write down income tax deductions or a Christmas list. The back page was for recommended reading. Now when someone says, "You must read this," Barbara writes down the title and it's at her fingertips the next time she is in a bookstore.

She laughed at herself as she shared her planner. "I sound so efficient and yet I know I'm not. It's just that the Lord has given me all this help. I depend on Him 100 percent. I know what I'm like without Him."

Then almost pensively she added, "What's more, the planner has shown me two things I hadn't known before about the Lord and time. Sometimes He asks me to put the plans aside and do something special for Him. Whenever this happens, I do it willingly because I've learned that when the special job is done I can trust Him to help me get every important thing on the list finished in far less time than it would have ordinarily taken.

"Another thing He's shown me is that when something comes up that is too big or too complicated for me to plan, than all I have to do is write it down and ask Him to work it into my time schedule wherever He thinks it is best." She shared her own experience of trying to develop a planner book like hers for the women who might want to send away for one instead of making their own.[1]

"It was a big project to write down everything the Lord

had shown me, everything I'd seen in similar books and to find the right Scriptures, then to plan it so it would be practical for everybody. I didn't know when I'd find the time to do it because of everything that had to be done first. I'd put it down on my To Do list and asked the Lord to help me find the time, but there I was the day before I was supposed to have it ready and it was still not started. I thought, 'I'll just have to humble myself and tell the Aglow editors that I didn't do it.' Then all of a sudden there was time, a whole lot of time. I sat down, and, with the Lord's help, the whole planning book flowed together in just a few hours without any interruptions.''

We, too, can let the planning that began with Barbara's need become the Lord's tool in our own lives. Whether we send away for the planner Barbara designed or make our own or purchase a similar one in a stationery store, a planner can help each of us: the single woman, the family woman, the organized, the disorganized. Everyone who wants to be a more efficient Christian woman today will benefit from the idea the Lord gave Barbara and which she has so willingly shared in detail with us.

11

Two
Great
Robberies

It was only about 9:30 that night when Mother came home from church. Her little mutt of a dog was yapping its head off, no doubt trying to warn her of the danger. "I'm coming, I'm coming," she called.

At the top of the stairs she stopped short. Papers and envelopes covered the floor. It looked like everything in the filing cabinet had been dumped out. What she saw next made her heart nearly stop, someone's tools on the floor! One word flashed to her mind, *burglars.* She let the dog out and fled downstairs and out the door to the greenhouse where Dad had stopped after putting the car away. She pounded on the door.

"Lorraine, what on earth?" Dad asked.

She was so frightened she couldn't even speak, but her mouth formed the word, "Robbery."

Eventually the police came and they all went into the house to see what was actually missing. They discovered that the burglars had taken the only valuable pieces my parents owned, two diamond rings from another generation. All their other pretty but worthless baubles were left in place.

The police told Mom and Dad that this was the twenty-eighth robbery in their area in two months. In every case only costly jewelry had been stolen. Obviously the work had been done by professionals who knew exactly what to take.

In the same way, there is much that the great robber of Christians, Satan, could steal from us. But because he, too, is a professional thief he searches through our accumulated valuables and tries to get away with one of our most important commodities, *our energy*. He knows that if he can rob us of this, our lives will be ineffective. Jesus said Satan's only purpose in coming is to steal, to slaughter and destroy (cp. Jn. 10:10). In stealing our energy he also steals *our time*. He knows one without the other is useless. Time doesn't do us any good if our energy is gone. Our energy won't get us anywhere if our time is wasted.

We've discovered many timesaving ways to thwart Satan's attempt to render our Christian lives useless. Let's talk about how we can make his attempt to steal our energy just as ineffective. *The number one loss of energy comes from worry.* Many people worry over everything.

Those who worry come in all shapes and sizes and degrees of worrying skill. Beginning worriers worry about the weather, about what happened yesterday and what will happen tomorrow.

Practiced worriers are good at money problems, personality problems or people around them and the mistakes they will make in the future.

Advanced worriers have a complete repertoire of worries. A teen-ager I know looked at the calendar in July and worried about whose turn it would be to do the dishes on Christmas. A mother can worry over a too-harsh punishment she dished out fifteen years ago. A grandmother can worry about the future of a grandchild who is being raised differently from the way she raised her children.

Whatever the cause, the woman who worries spends her energy and then her time as foolishly as a teen-ager who wastes all her money on a game of chance at the fair. The rest of the day lies ahead, but with her savings gone, so are her plans. When we blow our energy on worrying, no matter what we want to do with our day or our life, we have said good-bye to our accomplishments.

What does a Christian woman do about worry? Habits of worry are as hard to shed as habits of overeating. But as someone else has said, "The journey of a thousand miles begins with a single step." The Christian is fortunate because her first step is giving her worry to Jesus and letting Him deal with it.

When Satan piles worries on us until we are crippled under their weight, Jesus can, in an instant, dissolve the whole burden and make us free. He promised, "Come to me, all who labor and are heavy laden, and I will give you rest" (Matt. 11:28 RSV).

If any of the following are your worries, then take the first step to give them to Jesus for He has offered us a wonderful exchange:

> *Yesterday:* Dear Lord, in the past I've done some awful things and hurt someone badly. Jesus, I'm sorry; please forgive me. I give this worry over to You and I'm counting on Your promise to take it away.

> *Tomorrow:* There is something ahead of me tomorrow, Lord, that is so personally frightening that I can't face it without worry. Jesus, with Your help I can face anything. Give me the grace to trust You in my life and heal me of this attitude of worry.

> *Money:* I know that there is not going to be enough money, Father. I don't know how we will manage. Yet, Lord, You have said I could trust You. From this moment on, my money worries are in Your hands. With Your help, I will look to You instead of to myself.

> *Weather:* I know I worry about the rain and

snow all winter and the heat in summer. I worry
about slick roads and about plans being
changed. Okay, Lord, I'm going to give this
worry over to You. Please take it away and give
me peace in whatever situation I find myself.

Children: I can't help but worry about the
children. There is always something that one of
them is doing that is so disappointing. What
will happen to them? How will they ever be
responsible Christian adults? Jesus, this is a
worry I'm glad to give over to You. Please take
it and strengthen me to trust You in all things.

Husband: My husband is such a worry to me.
He's as foolish and as thoughtless as a child.
What will he do next? Jesus, this is not my
worry. I see now that I can trust You to work in
his life. I'm asking You to take this burden of
worry and exchange it for Your peace.

Prayers like these work. Everyone who has tried them
knows what it means to be free of worry. Unfortunately,
they don't always work once and for all. How wonderful it
would be if they did, but we know that Satan hates to give up.
As we surrender one worry, he will offer another.

Yet the victory over all these worries has already been
guaranteed by Jesus, and so we say each time, "Jesus, I give
this to You, this new little worry that just came, the worry I
didn't turn over to You yesterday. Help me to turn them all
over to You so I can keep my mind free to do the great things
You have planned with my time and energy today."

As a further antidote for getting out of the worry habit, I'd
like to share something that Rita Langdon, a Christian
woman in a close-by neighborhood, shared with me. Rita said
that she sought for two weeks to know God's will for her.
Then she heard the words in her heart, *"Think beautiful*

thoughts."

She replied, "Lord, that is not what I mean. I want to *do* something."

Again she heard the words, *"Think beautiful thoughts."*

The more she thought about it, the more she realized her mind had been full of worries and so she began with the Lord's help to think only beautiful thoughts. What a change it brought! "I feel so happy," she told me. "I'm coming into a deeper peace and although I've always loved my husband, I've found new ability to lay down my life for him. There is power in my life that I've never known that enables me to tell others about Jesus. Thinking beautiful thoughts has released me from the tyrant of worry" (Phil. 4:6-8).

If we will take every worrisome thought that Satan suggests and send it away and then let the Holy Spirit fill our minds with goodness, we will have a whole new world of peace and accomplishment waiting for us.

But as we've said before, Satan is a professional thief. If he can't worry us into wasting our time, then one of his next steps is to *divert our attention.* Diversion is one of his subtle tactics that seems to work well with Christians. It's not so much that we get talked into something we shouldn't do but that we let ourselves get talked out of doing what we know we should.

Michelle saw how her husband Jeff had been last place in her life and she determined that she would be the wife to him that God wanted her to be. For all the years of their marriage she had put everyone else's conversation ahead of his. She had had long, long chats with the neighbors, the garbage man, anyone at all after church. Meanwhile, Jeff had waited in the car, waited in the supermarket or changed his plans because she had left him babysitting too long while her talking went on and on.

When Michelle tried to change to find Jeff as interesting as she found others, she couldn't do it. Satan whispered in her ear, "He's so dull; he's not interested in talking to you anyway. Why waste your time?" And Michelle found herself agreeing instead of becoming the "friend" to Jeff she knew God wanted her to be.

Linda, a single gal, knew that since she had no husband or family the order for her life was prayer first, commitment to the Christian community second. After a great deal of prayer she decided to take some college courses in religious education so she could be of value in her parish church.

But Linda loved her television evenings so much, her studying for the new college classes wasn't getting done. "After this next program," she'd say. Then again, "Just one more program." Finally it would be too late to do anything but go wearily off to bed. Satan would tell her, "Don't be a fool, you're single. Your life is your own. Why don't you enjoy yourself tonight and study tomorrow instead?"

Marta was one of those women who was the first one to say she had order in her life. It was the kingdom of God first, her husband next, her two sons after that and then her volunteer work for the pastor last. For Marta, it was the work for the pastor that got in the way.

When two people approximately the same age of the opposite sex are together for long periods of time, it's very easy for the devil to interfere. Lust grew in Marta's mind towards her pastor. At first Satan whispered, "Wouldn't it be wonderful if you had married him instead? What would happen if you were marooned on a desert island with him?" Marta's imagination did the rest. As adultery was committed in her mind, Marta was diverted from being the Christian woman she was called to be. She knew that the answer was to quit her job, get as far away as possible from this man who was so tempting to her and get her life back into the order she pretended it was in. Again Satan whispered, "You're an adult; you can keep these feelings under control. You're doing a good Christian work; why should you quit?"

As each of these three women was diverted from what they were called by God to do by Satan's lies, their purposes, goals, priorities and plans meant nothing.

Fortunately, in time each discovered the threefold solution for temptation.

One, we cannot argue with Satan. With each suggestion

he sends we should give no thought to it but calmly turn to Jesus and say, "I Love You. I Want Your will to be done in my life."

Two, we must make a heart's decision to change. A vague resolve is not enough; there must be a definite resolution to turn to God and to be the person He want us to be.

Three, we must not attempt change in our own strength. We must go before God and admit our own sinfulness and helpfulness to do anything about our weakness. Then after we have asked His forgiveness, knowing that He gives it gladly, we can ask Jesus to be our strength and free us from Satan. Jesus, who loves us so much even when we have made ourselves ugly with sin, will hear and answer a desperate heartfelt prayer to be the person we know He wants us to be.

Michelle, Linda and Marta all found that Jesus is the only answer to Satan's diversion tactic. Each restated her purpose and asked the Lord to be her strength in working out her goals, priorities and plans.

Michelle's husband tells her he has never been so happy. She wonders how she could have been so blind to his needs. Linda says she has strength that she never guessed possible to turn the television set off and study instead.

Marta, after weeks of tears and a struggle, at last determined in her heart to leave her job. With Jesus' help in the midst of her own helplessness she walked away from the man who had so much appeal. Right now she still doesn't have another job. She has times of loneliness, but her heart is at peace. She says that no one can know how wonderful it is to be in the place that the Lord wants her to be until she has lived through the pain of letting Satan lead her out of God's will.

Unlike the two diamond rings stolen from my mother, the call the Lord has on our lives is priceless. Let's ask Jesus to be our guard against worry and our protector from Satan's diversions.

12

The Urgent versus The Important

It still embarrasses me to remember that day I spent so much time cleaning the house before a photographer came to take my picture that I was too tense to work well with her.

A neighbor tells of the time she spent so much effort in decorating for a luncheon to welcome new Christians she was too weary to talk enthusiastically to them when they arrived.

Many of us can remember Christmases when we spent so much energy in preparation that when the great and holy day finally arrived, we were so exhausted we just wished it would end quickly.

In each of these cases, the urgent was confused with the important. The important items in the above examples were the picture-taking session, the new Christians and the Lord's birthday. The urgent were a clean house, clever decorations and holiday trimming. *Every time the urgent is put first, the important takes second place.*

I've confused the urgent and the important many times but the last time I did so still lives vividly in my memory. I was at the last important stage of my *Aglow Magazine* work when a friend called the office and said, "It's extremely urgent that you drop everything and come with me and pray for Sally."

"What's the matter?"

"It's her husband; he has disappeared again and she's desperate."

It was truly a dilemma for me. Should I drop my work and put the magazine schedule behind? I had done quite a bit of arranging of my children and meals in order to have this block of time but should I ever turn down a plea to pray with someone in need? Which was important? Quickly I prayed about it and the answer that the Holy Spirit seemed to give me at that time was, *Continue on with what you are doing because the visible work of the Church is as important as the invisible.*

But my friend insisted that Sally needed me to pray with her and since I didn't want to appear unspiritual, I said I'd go. After the three of us prayed together, my friend prayed and prayed and prayed some more. Then Sally insisted that we stay for lunch.

When finally we said goodbye I knew I'd made a mistake. My friend should have gone by herself. I should have stayed with my work. Now I had put several people behind in their plans. I wondered how I could have been so foolish. Why hadn't I waited until tomorrow? Surely she'd need someone then, too.

This area is so confusing that if we don't know which is important and which is urgent, our friends will frequently urge us to do the urgent.

Estelle was young and vulnerable and a friend had insisted that she go out and solicit for some charitable cause, even inferring she wouldn't be much of a Christian if she didn't go. Estelle left her three young children alone, and while she was gone they tried to make toast. When it burned, they attempted to get the piece out of the toaster with a fork. The fork hit a wire and her two-year-old was so badly shocked from the burn and, I imagine, so frightened at being alone and in pain that it was two years and much therapy before he said another word.

Sometimes only experience teaches us the difference.

"It's urgent that you help out with the bazaar," someone told my friend Martha Hickman. But with the wisdom that comes from being over forty, Martha replied, "No, it's not urgent at all. I'm not a bazaar person. I don't like to sew frilly things or make clever decorations." She also knew that if she took on the bazaar work, her important work as the president of a Women's Aglow Fellowship would suffer and so would the women who counted on her.

The one who always was able to separate the urgent from the important was Jesus. He was told that it was *urgent* that He go to Bethany because Lazarus was dying. Jesus knew it was more important that He go later and raise Lazarus from the dead.

Jesus was hailed as a mighty king as He rode into Jerusalem on a donkey; throngs laid palm branches and cloaks at His feet and shouted hosannahs. Yet this urgent display of favor did not alter the important work He had come to do. He wasn't sidetracked. He had come into the world to save us, not by earthly kingships but by laying down His life. Before going to Gethsemane we hear Him say, "I have finished the work which thou gavest me to do" (John 17:4).

After only a three-year ministry, how could He make such a statement? While a few had found salvation, thousands still knew nothing about Jesus. Many "urgent" human needs remained unmet; yet He knew He had finished God's work.

How can we decide in our own lives which is important and which is urgent? To begin with we can ask our family's opinions about their needs. Martha Hickman decided to check with her husband about what was really important to him that she should do. His reply was simply, "A smile when I come home at night and pecan pie on Christmas." That eliminated quite a few urgent things from Martha's life.

Perhaps we can reevaluate some of the work around the house. Mary Bouma, a practical writer-homemaker advises,

"Every bed does not necessarily have to be changed every week. A lot depends on the color of the sheets, the size of the bed, and the person sleeping it it.'"

Time consultant Alan Lakein suggests that one of the best ways to find time for important things is by reducing the unimportant jobs. He counsels:

> Definite [superfluous tasks] include rearranging a pile of magazines, inventorying the freezer (when you just did it last month and nothing has changed significantly in the interim), mopping the kitchen floor just before the children come home on a rainy day . . . You can probably think of many other items that are too trivial to do, or will settle themselves by the passage of time, or are best forgotten unless there is a demand from an outside source . . .
>
> If you can let the dusting, washing, filing, or checking go one more day, then let it. You will have spent less of your life dusting, filing, and washing.[2]

Here is another way to divide the urgent from the important. "Would you like to be able to read 50,000 words in a minute?" James T. McCay asks. "There are many times when it is easy to do this when you know how. All you have to be able to do is recognize within one minute that a 50,000 word book does not fit your purposes and decide not to read it."[3]

Most importantly when distinguishing between the urgent and the important it is good to get an overview of the whole picture. We can do this by using the personal time investment worksheet on the next page which has been shared with us by the Managing Your Time people. Following are the instructions that come with the worksheet:

> Make a list of a number of things you see yourself doing. They could be at work, at home, your job, your recreation, however you see yourself spending major blocks of time, say more than thirty minutes a day. Now go down the three columns and evaluate how you feel about that area of expenditure, too little, just right, too

**PERSONAL TIME INVESTMENT
ANALYSIS WORKSHEET**

A World Vision MARC MANAGEMENT SERIES
Missions Advanced Research & Communication Center
919 West Huntington Drive
Monrovia, California 91016

HOW AM I SPENDING MY TIME? Note anything that comes to mind, home, business, family, spiritual life, etc.	How Much Do I Spend?		
	Too Little	Just Right	Too Much

much. Put a mark in the appropriate column.[4]

When our list is completed, let's ask ourselves which of these items are really important and which are only urgent (and which are neither). If we are spending too much time on some things that are not important and too little on something that is, then we will have a good starting point for change. Separating the urgent from the important has the potential of finding new areas of time for us every day.

13

Time Off for the Cook

Our family found that going off to the beach for part of the summer brought us the leisure that refreshes all year long. The first few years that we packed up the family and rented a cabin at the beach I loved it. I loved the peaceful afternoons for reading, the long summer sunsets, the quiet and relaxation I couldn't find at home.

Then gradually, although I didn't understand why, I began to hate those few weeks of the summer more than any others. But as our family grew, a cabin at the beach seemed the only sensible vacation. Bill looked forward to it, the children talked of it all year and since only I dreaded it, it was silly not to go.

Then one vacation evening, as I was sitting on the beach watching a sunset that I was almost too weary to enjoy and fretting about my dislike of what everyone called the "perfect time," it suddenly dawned on me why I was so out of step. The answer was so simple I wondered why I hadn't seen it before. Those first vacations that I had loved were when the children were small. We had played simple games in the morning, eaten simple meals and the children had not only napped in the afternoon but had gone to bed exhausted at night, leaving **Bill and me the long summer evenings to ourselves.**

How different it was now with a cabin full of children and hungry teen-agers who always seemed to have a hungry friend as well. There were still the early mornings with the little children, but no such things as quiet afternoons. No such things as three simple meals, no such things as long peaceful evenings for Bill and me together. Indeed, we usually turned in before some of the kids did. I hated those weeks at the beach because my subconscious mind was still geared for leisure and, of course, there was very little of it to be had.

From that day on I looked at our family vacation with new eyes. My purpose changed from leisure for myself to that of giving the family a good time and, in particular, giving Bill a change of pace from his busy workaday world. Although I never really enjoyed the beach wholeheartedly again, knowing I had not come for my own leisure took away the restless, uneasy feeling I had begun to associate with being there.

Still, I knew I needed leisure, too. So I planned for it, setting goals I knew could be reached: theater with Bill, lunch with one of my daughters or a friend, a hot soaky bath with a book. Others might want to play tennis or golf or create clever handcrafts. Whatever, leisure should be part of the purpose of every woman. We should give it the same test of goals, priorities and planning that we give everything else that comes into our lives.

We must think of leisure as something we do for God's purpose. It is His ally as well as ours. We do not work in order to have leisure. We spend leisure in order that we might get on with our work. Charlie Shedd observes:

> When our work is God's work, then taking time for refreshment so that we can do our job better is something we have to consider.
>
> Our Heavenly Father never gives us too much to do. Men will. We assign ourselves an overload, but never the Lord. He knows what He wants from each of us, and there is plenty of time in His day for things essential to His plan. We do Him a grave injustice when we fall into the habit of compulsive overwork.[1]

The industrial planners tell us that a time away from our work allows us to return to our job with a greater level of efficiency. As a result of their research into leisure, short coffee breaks and compulsory two-week vacations have become an integral part of the American business world.

Too often we think we don't deserve leisure or that our Christian work is so important that we don't dare take a minute off. If anyone needed to sit a spell with her feet up and become refreshed it was our Christian-work oriented, cranky Aunt Betty. To her, leisure and sloth were synonymous. Life was too serious, the work too important. As children we hated visiting her because Aunt Betty never stopped bustling or telling us how much there was to do. Her canning, her Sunday school class, her cleaning, her missionary work were all grim and scheduled. On Sunday, the day of rest in her small Bible-belt community, Aunt Betty had a way of doing "only what was necessary" to such an extent that it took all day.

Mother would say, "Come, Betty, sit on the porch for awhile. The evening sky is beautiful."

Aunty Betty would sigh indignantly and remind all the porch sitters, "Someone has to do the work around here. Heaven only knows Sunday supper doesn't appear by magic." The screen door would bang and before long the other aunts on the porch would guiltily find their way to the kitchen, too.

The acceptance of leisure must come before we can take time from our work. We must be convinced that time for ourselves is time well spent. Someone who I think has a good sense of leisure is Sister Carolyn, the hardworking nun in charge of our church's religious education program. She says that she she loves to sit on the beach and dig her feet into the sand and do nothing. She confided as we drank coffee in her tiny apartment, "It may look like I'm wasting valuable time but actually sitting on the sand is, for me, a time for gaining back some of the strength it takes to be a nun in America today." Yet it is not something she does while the Lord's work goes undone but something she plans for, an important part of the whole woman.

Jo Stanley is one of those wonderful women who gives people like Erma Bombeck an inferiority complex. Jo has raised nine children of her own as well as various grandchildren and neighborhood children. She keeps the books for her husband's business, bakes and decorates wedding cakes for everyone in the family, and is always there in church activities and in every crisis. I asked her, "Jo, don't you ever take time off for yourself?"

"Oh yes," she answered.

"When?"

She replied that often between midnight and one in the morning she sits and reads and thinks and prays. When the house is quiet she feels it's a shame to waste that quiet in sleeping. So she plans it as a time of renewal in her busy life. As with Sister Carolyn, it is a leisure that refreshes her for her work.

For some women leisure is a reward. Just as Sunday leisure is a reward for six days of work the restfulness of old age can be a reward for our work-filled lives. Mother tells a story of an afternoon when she was bustling around the church getting ready for a banquet. It was hurry and do this, rush and do that until the pace of all the workers was frantic. Damp strands of hair hung over Mother's forehead as she poked flowers into vases and carried trays of plates.

On the sidelines of all the activity was an ancient Chinese grandmother sitting serenely, her hands in her lap. Seeing her, Mother stopped and pushed her hair back with her arm and greeted the old woman, "Oh, my, what a busy day this is, Mrs. Lew. I wonder why we ever allow ourselves to get so caught up in our preparation."

Mrs. Lew nodded and agreed. From the vantage point of her age she probably did see how foolish all the running around was. With an encouraging little smile she patted Mother's hand, "Don't feel bad," she said, "someday you will be old, too."

The idea of leisure is as old as creation. God made the world in six days and on the seventh day, Genesis tells us, He rested (Gen. 2:2). Growing up, we took this example literally and did not plan work on Sunday. Once when Wanda, a junior in college, put in a hem on Sunday, Mother was shocked. "My child," she said, giving in to one of the adages that has been around for generations, "any work you do on Sunday comes out with your nose on Monday."

"Mother is so old-fashioned," we laughed. But the next day Wanda caught the hem of her dress on a car door and the repair took her an afternoon. Our eyes met as we remembered Mother's warning.

Coincidence? I suppose, but I've had many such coincidences. It does seem to me that the rest of the week goes better when the family keeps Sunday as a day set apart from work.

There are many women who find that planning leisure is more difficult than planning their work. Throughout our lifetime, leisure comes in packages of all sizes and shapes. When someone comes by with a gift for us we don't say, "I'll wait until the third week of May when I'm not so rushed to open this." No. We rip off the wrapping, open the box and enjoy the gift inside. And so it should be with leisure.

Sometimes, it's best just to take leisure a little bit at a time when the moment arrives. One tiny package of leisure was suggested by Marabel Morgan, author of *The Total Woman,* a sensuous 5 p.m. bubble bath for women to get themselves fragrantly clean and ready for their husband's arrival home.[2]

A weekend packet of leisure has come to many people in the form of a Christian retreat. When the children were all little I used to count the days until our church's yearly silent retreat. Imagine coming from a noisy household into three days of silence! Now there are teen-age retreats, married couples retreats, Women's Aglow Fellowship retreats, denominational retreats, so many that it seems all of Christendom sees the advantage in taking a break from even the Lord's work to consider the Lord Himself.

A weekly package of leisure came into my life during one going-on-forty pregnancy. My doctor prescribed one evening out away from the family each week. Bill and I took this advice literally and spent every Friday night for over six months going to dinner or the theater (at that time Bill wasn't wild about prayer meetings).

We really couldn't afford it, but we did it anyway, and often we have said how glad we were that we took the time. It added a richness to our communication we thought was lost and a new vigor to the lives of two people who thought they were a little too old to be parents again.

There are yearly packages of leisure to be opened. A friend, Maggie, an older single gal, saves enough money to take a yearly Caribbean cruise during her "two weeks with pay." Instead, she takes those two weeks off and works in a Chicago orphanage to give the nuns there a little relief. She said it's always hard making the adjustment from office to nursery but each summer she comes away feeling the time was well worth the effort. For her, it brings memories that last the whole year through.

And leisure, like gifts, sometimes comes in a surprise package.

One morning when Danny was not yet two years old we drove the older children to school and started out on the rounds of Thursday errands: grocery shopping, cleaners, post office, hardware store. It was fall. The sun shone through the half-clothed trees and made lace cutouts with the leaves that had fallen on the grass below. Deciding on the long way around, I drove by the lake to get one last glimpse of the sailboats that would soon be dry-docked during the coming cold. We paused as a parade of ducks waddled across the road in front of the car. "Look, Danny, look at the ducks."

Danny clapped his hands and let his tongue experiment with the new sound. "Duck, duck." He grinned at me, asking with his eyes if he had said it right.

On an impulse I pulled the car to the side of the road. "Come on, Danny. Let's see if we can see those ducks for ourselves." I took his hand and together we brought up the rear of the duck procession like giant majorettes at a pygmy parade. Across the road, down a slope and onto the beach we followed them until the water's edge stopped us short.

"Duck," Danny said, sure of his new word now. Together, we walked along feeling the autumn sun, listening to the hoarse quacks coming from off the shore. Sometimes Danny ran ahead and sometimes he touched base by taking my hand for a minute. The morning was passing and yet neither one of us wanted to turn back. I decided to skip the hardware store and go to the post office tomorrow. I walked on and on savoring the moment, knowing it would pass and never come this way again. Who could care about the cleaners? Did it matter a bit on a beautiful day like this if the raincoats were waterproofed? As for the grocery shopping, it would get done eventually.

A breeze came up off the water and suddenly, despite the sun, the air was chilled as it should be in autumn. "Let's go back, Danny."

Obediently Danny reversed his steps to match mine. We had come a long way. Sometimes he danced beside me; part of the way I carried him. He repeated with continuous excitement, "Duck, duck."

When we got back to the car the morning was gone, but it had not slipped into the oblivion of a thousand others but, rather, into a little niche in my memory. Whenever I see a mother and her toddler, I remember Danny and the ducks and our morning of leisure in the sun.

Did Jesus take leisure time? He had so much to do and so little time to do it in one would think that He would have spent His three years of public ministry going at a frantic pace. Yet the Bible tells us that He went away to rest with His disciples. Often we see Him slipping away to pray after a day spent with the press of the crowds. We read that He took time with children doing nothing except enjoying them. He passed time just visiting at the Bethany home of Lazarus. He went to a wedding feast and ate with sinners and remarkably, all of this time of leisure was spent in the Father's will.

So, too, in our lives leisure does not mean taking time off

from God's plan for our lives but refreshing ourselves for the work He has for us to do. We see that leisure, like work, has many faces. It can be planned, it can be unexpected. It can masquerade as work, and sometimes work acts as though it were our leisure. We can ignore it or we can use it.

Where does leisure fit into the plans of a woman who would set sail for new lands? It is part of the rich green and brown of the planning. For it, the whole woman will go adventuring, the woman who has learned that leisure time can prepare her for the work that lies ahead.

14

Why Not Let George Do It?

As a girl I once discovered a wonderfully efficient, totally dishonest method of getting my assigned Saturday work done rapidly. On Saturday mornings, my job was to clean the living room; Wanda's was to clean the dining room.

While Wanda slept, I slipped down to the room that was my responsibility, picked up all the papers, coffee cups and the horde of miscellaneous junk and piled it all on the dining room table. Then I listened to the radio until everyone else was up. After breakfast I vacuumed end dusted the living room and went to play. Meanwhile, Wanda was so completely bogged down by everything that had to be put away, it was noon and many tears later before she was finally finished.

My method worked so well that the following Saturday I used it again, except this time I overplayed my hand. My parents had had company the night before, and I took the teapot, the dessert dishes and teacups and plopped them on the dining room table along with everything else that had cluttered the front room that morning.

This time Wanda caught on and protested with a mighty yowl. Mother was furious at my dishonesty and hard-heartedness toward my sister. As a result, I was assigned

Wanda's work as well as my own. When mother heaved a sigh and left the room Wanda stuck out her tongue and I snarled that she was nothing but a brat.

Wanda and I also had to help with the canning, keep the yard mowed and do the evening dishes together. Even on the best days this last job was a never-ending battle.

"You didn't get that clean. Do it again."

"Mom, she's being picky."

"You wipe the table; it's your turn."

"It is not; you never do anything."

One memorable evening when the quarreling reached a crescendo, Mother came into the kitchen, her eyes glaring. "Get out of here, both of you. I'm so sick and tired of your bickering. I'll do the dishes myself."

We were delighted, of course, but our aprons weren't even off before my father loomed in the doorway and roared, "Lorraine, you'll do no such thing. That work is their responsibility and they have to do it."

We had never heard Dad scold Mother before and we were horrified. He whisked her off to the front room and Wanda and I, startled beyond words, gave the dishes the best washing they had ever had, even cleaning the hated coffee pot and the frying pan we had already stashed in the oven. For once we did it without quarreling.

I offer all this for one reason, to give a glimpse of how difficult children's work can be for parents. Sometimes kids are so quarrelsome that it is ten times easier for the parents to do their work than delegate it to a bunch of arguing complainers. But we parents need to stick with it. In Wanda's and my case, it wasn't too much later in those troubled postwar times that we both earned much of our own way working in people's homes. We were able to get the jobs because, although we had certainly tried not to, we had learned the fundamentals of work.

Today the question I hear most often is, "Does children's work really help?" The answer is yes. It helps you and even more it helps them. Let's first talk about the benefits in saved time to us. Most important, delegating work extends the results of our own work. For instance, say there are two hours before dinner to get a box of peaches into the freezer. This is almost impossible without help, but if one child peels and another slices, no matter how much extra fuss their work takes and no matter how sloppy their work is, the peaches will get done on time.

Or suppose Bill should call and say he is bringing home guests. There is one hour to do a number of things that two minutes before hadn't looked too important. Again, it's the kids who can put away the bikes in the driveway, wash the fingerprints off the picture window and reset the table with a tablecloth and napkins.

Alec MacKenzie, the famed time expert, says that it is a fallacy to say of a subordinate's job, "I can do it better myself." "Actually," he says, "a subordinate's work should leave you free to do something else better."[1]

So it is in a household. Back in the house on Twelfth Avenue, Bill Jr. and Dave were eight and ten when they took turns doing dishes after dinner and what a terrible job they did! Water everywhere, the frying pan never really done well and the counter smeared instead of cleaned. I could have done it better myself, of course, but one of the purposes of their work was to free me to feed the baby and bathe the little ones. Then, when Bill and Dave were prayed with and tucked into bed, I could go back to the kitchen and undo the damage, grateful that I wasn't starting the whole kitchen cleanup from scratch.

Another way children's work frees us to do a better job is when we absolutely must meet a deadline with another project. Our friends, the Zipp family, had seven girls in a row. Their mother bought yardage by the bolt each spring to make seven new coats for Easter. But in order for her to do this, the girls took care of all the housework.

Follow-up is important in teaching a child or anyone a job. As the children grew older, instead of doing their work over, I called them back to do it themselves. I don't know who hated it worse. They complained and grumbled and acted persecuted until it would have been easier to overlook their carelessness, but eventually they learned to do it right the first time. And when they did it right, it was important to seek them out and compliment them on a worthy job.

Mr. Mackenzie also says that fear of being disliked keeps managers from correcting the mistakes of their subordinates.[2] Mr. Mackenzie, let me tell you that this fear of dislike absolutely paralyzes some of us parents. It is miserable to see a twelve-year-old crying crocodile tears into the kitchen sink because she is missing a chance to go with her friends who don't have such awful parents.

It takes courage, the courage only the Holy Spirit can give, to go down to a teen-ager's room and bring him back to the scene of the half-done or not-done-at-all job and stand over him until he gets it done. It takes laying-down-your-life heroism to walk over to a basketball game and announce that the center and forward have forgotten chores at home.

But, as Mr. Mackenzie's survey showed that the managers who expected high quality work from their employees were better liked than those who took everyone else's work home on the weekend,[3] so, I am sure, it is with families. Children and teen-agers respect a parent who not only makes regulations but sees that they are carried out.

Regardless of what is said about forbidden fruit tasting better, a basketball game played with the knowledge that the work is done has to be more enjoyable than playing with the knowledge that Mom and the work are back waiting, and Mom isn't too patient. In fact, learning to work is so important that Proverbs 13:24 which reads, "If you refuse to discipline your son, it proves you don't love him . . ." (TLB), can be paraphrased to say: "When a parent takes precious time to teach a job done right, it proves her love."

Another tip from Mr. Mackenzie: "Make clear what's expected; the hasty order given to save time usually doesn't."[4] No doubt any parent who has discovered delegation has caught on to this one the hard way. To an adult, "Paint the lawn furniture," implies putting away the paint and soaking the brush when you are done. Not so with a nonadult. Unless spelled out, "Paint the lawn furniture," means, "Stop and go somewhere else when the last board is painted."

Once when Bill confronted a teen-ager with a can of paint the baby had tipped over in the driveway, he looked hurt that his father had mentioned it. "It's not my fault. You didn't say to put the paint away." When Bill mentioned that the boy also hadn't painted the bottom of the picnic table, the hurt look returned. "But you didn't say to paint the bottom."

With dishes it's, "But you didn't say to rinse out the dish-pan," with emptying the garbage, "But you didn't say to put the lid back on the garbage can," or with mowing the lawn, "But you didn't say the strip by the garage."

Also in working with our children there are a few "musts." I've learned every one of these the hard way by trial and error, it seems. I pass them on hoping they will benefit someone just beginning.

Allow mistakes. There is a vast difference between disobedience and mistaken judgment. A pair of new levis in with the sheets is a mistake and no one knows it more than a teen-age washerwoman who discovers what she has done. Confusing the Windex and the hair spray is a mistake. Boiling jam in a kettle that is too small can be a horrible mistake. But we learn from mistakes and not only do we learn but we grow up a little each time we correct our own. Mistakes are a part of the overall challenge to everyone and so it is with our children. They need to clean up after their errors but not to be scolded for them.

Be prepared to compromise. "Mom, I have to be at school at 6 p.m. tonight. Can I do that job tomorrow?" Or, from me after a child has struggled too long with a job he really wasn't ready for, "You've worked hard enough on that. I'll finish it for you." Or when Joe, who for a whole year couldn't find a friend finally found a nice one, "Joe, you just go ahead and play. Someone else will do your work, and, honey, have a good time today."

Respect their time schedule. It's wrong to interrupt a child's work. "Katy, will you go to the store and finish picking up the toys when you get home?" is unfair. Katy may have her plans all laid out and what's more when she gets back all the toys she's picked up may be out again. "Get out there right now and sweep the patio," can frustrate a child who has made specific plans to do the patio as soon as it's in the shade. Perhaps the worst is asking a child who has finished his work ahead of the others and is curled up with a book, to do something else that is not in the emergency class.

Let them have fun work. The delegation that saves us time doesn't necessarily mean delegating all the "grub" work. Nancy Osburn, a young Christian mother in our neighborhood, has a job jar for her young son. After school he takes a slip of paper out and does the job printed on it. Mostly it's the usual empty-the-garbage, clean-your-room type work, but sometimes he finds a slip with a job that is fun: "Sharpen all the pencils," "Put up the badminton kit and play a game of badminton with me." Once in a while the job jar yields a surprise, "Share a popsicle with your brother," or "No work today; you deserve a rest," or "It's raining; do the puzzle Dad bought on Saturday."

Children's work can definitely decrease our own, especially after the ground rules are in effect. The timesaving can be enormous, but what does work do for them? First, work keeps them from being bored. A couple of hours of work on a Saturday or summer vacation morning makes the afternoon that much more enjoyable. Children without morning work can be all played out and restless by noon. This way the day actually doesn't begin for them until after lunch.

Work develops a sense of worth. Children and teen-agers whose work is really needed feel good about themselves and the contribution they are making to the family. Teen-agers with vital home responsibilities have a far higher sense of self-worth than those who give little of themselves to the running of their homes. Another proverb that fits is this: "The man who knows right from wrong and has good judgment and common sense is happier than the man who is immensely rich" (Prov. 3:13, 14 TLB). To it I would add, "The teen-ager who is responsible for something important is happier than the teen-ager who is rich with nothing to do." (I doubt, however, that there is a teen-ager around who would admit to this.)

Work can make more mature Christians of our children. If they can learn to do a hard piece of work, then the opportunity of doing something hard for the kingdom of God will not be turned away from so easily.

While all this advice may be great for a young family just getting started, what can be done about older children who have never had to take responsibilities, or an older child who used to help but now refuses? I would suggest that the key to successful delegation of work is the same for young or old, willing or unwilling. The door to cooperative workers is opened with praise. Sincere praise for the smallest job works wonders. For a reluctant worker, why not ask something small, something not too grubby and then reward that work with appreciation? From there go on to something a little more complex, especially work that obviously benefits the family, and sincerely praise the efforts.

At one time we had a teen-ager, Michelle, living with us who would absolutely not help. Finally we realized that she was so afraid she'd fail that she wouldn't attempt anything. It was through her that I learned to give small tasks at which she could not fail but that would be a contribution to the household She started by putting napkins at each place at dinner. When we found she was artistic, she became the one to arrange the flowers for the table, rearrange the cupboards or frost the cupcakes. Gradually, her self-confidence built up until she could handle an ordinary job with great satisfaction.

The first time we get a teen-ager to help us may not be the time to have him redo a job no matter how sloppily he's done it. Sensitive young people take criticism too personally. "Thank you for what you've done," may be the best response to give to a teen-ager who has done his best.

Sometimes when one considers all the pain and hassle it takes to get kids to do their work, it would seem that requiring jobs would eventually make them hate work. Actually the opposite is true. My father, who began plowing fields in Oklahoma at age seven until his shoulders and back ached, is still a mighty worker at age seventy-four. Many times I've come home and found the girls starting dinner or the boys straightening up the front room or someone else taking *everything* out of the rec room and cleaning it from scratch. This from kids who still balk at being assigned a job.

We've heard the proverb, "Train up a child in the way he should go: and when he is old, he will not depart from it (Prov. 22:6 KJV). We usually take this to mean spiritually and morally. Perhaps it means in a daily run of events as well. Children who learn to work at home are an asset on the job market. Bill Jr., now an accountant, put himself through college working in a restaurant. Dave is now doing the same. Mary Therese went to junior college on what she earned at a Kentucky Fried Chicken restaurant. All tell of those who came to work and lasted only a week or a day or even two hours on the job because they had never learned to work at home.

Whatever inroads we make, the child, the teen-ager, the young man or woman who learns to work, no matter how trying for himself or his mother, is far more liberated than the person who has never learned to apply himself. So is the mother who painfully taught the lessons and reaped the rewards of children who add to her time by helping with the work.

15

How to Beat the 4:30 Syndrome

Ethel Kennedy says that in the beginning of her marriage she had planned not to hire a cook but just enjoy cooking for her new husband and herself. But the first meal she put together became so involved with gourmet vegetables that when Bobby asked her, "Where's the meat?" Ethel blushed and admitted that she had forgotten all about a main course. The story goes that her husband firmly insisted that she hire a cook and that Ethel gladly complied.

I doubt that few of us, given the same chance, would have done differently. Is there anything in our lives as time and energy-consuming as getting dinner on the table seven nights a week? Yet it has to be done. The idea that the way to a man's heart is through his stomach has been bandied about for so many generations there has to be truth in it. Our husbands, if we want them to be all that husbands should be, have to be fed as well as possible and on time. Our teen-agers need that balanced dinner on time just as our little ones do.

The evening meal, year in and year out, is one of the great sacrifices a woman makes and perhaps the most unappreciated. Yet it pays the biggest dividends. Everything else being equal, families who can count on dinner on time will have fewer problems and much greater solidarity than families whose dinner is unplanned, vague or haphazard.

What's more, as we will see in a few minutes, dinner and dishes can provide us with two of the greatest opportunities we'll ever have to grow spiritually and walk more closely with the Lord.

Yet the 4:30 syndrome hits us all. We hate to get started. We haven't the energy. We think of women who are preparing to go out to beautiful restaurants for dinner and ask ourselves why we must always think up something for dinner, cook it, serve it and clean up after it. I remember the envy I felt when my friend, Virginia, said of her trip to Hawaii, "It was grand. The biggest decision I had to make all day was what to order for dinner."

The evening meal is important, we know that, but it can be so difficult that *planning the time for it* may be the only answer to achieving it. Using the backward planning method we learned in chapter 9 gives us the tool we need to do the job.

The *purpose* is obvious: our family needs nourishment as well as a set time to come together as a unit.

The *goal* is dinner at six o'clock (or five o'clock or eight o'clock) every night of the week.

However, as we learned from Barbara's planner, planning doesn't begin at 4:30 as the dinner hour closes in. It actually begins when we sit down with our husbands or our budget (or both) and figure out how much money we can spend on food. For, in order to cook dinner seven nights a week, we must have groceries. Before we can buy groceries we need a menu and before we can plan a menu we need to know how much money we can spend.

Meals begin with a set sum of money. It doesn't make sense to plan a menu we can't afford. A T-bone steak is great only as long as there is food on the table the rest of the week. The allotted amount of food money we have will tell us at a glance. Often the evening paper prints a recipe for an economy casserole that takes so many ingredients not found on my shelves that it is not economical at all for me.

When Bill and I were first married our food allowance was

$8.00 a week; three children later, it was $23.00. I remember when it went to $32.00 and now it's more than double that and the challenge to stay within it with spiraling prices is more difficult than ever. Whenever I feel sorry for myself I think of my friend, Margie, who with the same size family, can only spend half of what I do.

So let's talk about menu planning for a week at a time. I have a friend, Louise, who shops once a month for eighteen children and *never* goes back to the store for anything. That's terrific—it's something to aim for but not something to start with. Another friend, Amy, shops daily. She picked up the habit in Europe where a different life-style makes daily shopping a must. But for American housewives daily grocery shopping is a luxury of time most of us can ill afford. Our time must be budgeted like our money and shopping each day is as extravagant as a $300 blouse.

Once we know our weekly budget, we can plan our meals. As we already know, a weekly shopping schedule means a menu prepared in advance. A bride will want to write out total menus. The experienced shopper need only plan her dinners. My own menu planning begins on Friday, and it goes something like this:

> **Friday** — This is a holdover from the days when Friday meant fish to Catholic families. Now it is convenient and it may mean something as economical as red snapper or as much fun as the rainbow trout Grandpa caught last summer.

> **Saturday** — Hamburgers. It is such an interrupted day we need an easy meal.

> **Sunday** — Chicken or pot roast. That's traditional and children love tradition.

> **Monday** — Soybean meat substitute (texturized vegetable protein). Now this could be

pizza or tacos or Hawaiian meatballs[1]. We discovered that if Americans were to reduce their meat consumption by only 10 percent for one year, it would free for human consumption at least 12 million tons of grain, enough to feed 60 million grain eaters and help prevent famine in India.[2] So the switch to soybean meat substitute has had meaning for our family. It doesn't taste as good as meat, but there is a reason for doing it.[3]

Tuesday — Spaghetti and meatballs. Again soybean meat substitute can be substituted for part of the hamburger.

Wednesday — Liver. I don't get any cheers for this.

Thursday — Meat Loaf. Or something that will go into the oven while I'm finishing up the shopping.

A mental inventory of salad ingredients, vegetables, breakfast cereal, lunch-making ingredients and desserts makes up the rest of the list. Even with a well-stocked freezer, menu planning is a must, or the steaks will be gone too soon leaving only soup bones and no money for more. Experience has made shopping easy for me. It also has shown me not to shop without planning first.

Of course, every week is different. Sometimes we can afford steak and sometimes we have soybean meat substitute several times. A happy dessert works wonders on a budget day. A simple dessert is fine for an extravagant meal. (Bill's father was a German baker and, when Bill was growing up, dinner included several desserts. Bill still thinks the dessert is an integral part of every meal.) Some may think my menus are too austere, others will read them wistfully, thinking them grand. I offer them only as an example of a simple, preshopping menu.

Going to the store is something I used to dread every week until one day as I shopped with Wanda I told her how I felt about it. She stopped halfway through the turnstile and said, "How can you? It's such a privilege. American supermarkets are the envy of everyone around the world. American abundance is an impossible dream to women who have only a handful of rice to feed their half-starved family." As we seated our toddlers in our grocery carts she added, "Every time I pull up in front of a grocery store I say, 'Thank you, God, for the privilege of shopping.' " She made her point.

Even after we have figured our food budgets, planned our meals and shopped for the groceries, the great challenge still is getting dinner on the table on time. I mentioned that my married daughter Mary Therese, begins dinner in the morning. She babysits two little toddlers, so with her own baby she cares for three under two years of age. She says the day gets more hectic as it goes along, but as long as dinner is started she stays on top of it. Katie Fortune, executive editor of Aglow Publications, often puts her dinner on in a slow-cooking electric pot in the morning and it's ready when she comes home at night. Kitty Silvernale, a mother of twelve, all still at home, says that fixing dinner is part of the breakfast cleanup. She claims she wouldn't know how to clean up her kitchen without preparing another meal.

At our house this whole matter of dinner on time day in and day out, begins long before 4:30. Every afternoon after getting one boy off to kindergarten and the other one down for his nap, I work at my desk until the older children come in from school. From that point on, except for grocery shopping day, my plans call for being in the kitchen. It's a combination of listening to someone's reading, giving spelling words, sharing a cup of tea with my daughters, making cookies or a salad, or peeling potatoes. I don't plan housework, telephone calls or even any more work at my desk.

Although dinner preparation can take two or three hours

when it's done this way, there is more to it than just that. It's the good feeling a family gets of Mom's being in the kitchen and available and the good feeling that dinner is under way, even if it's only soybean meat substitute. More important, this is what works for me at this time with my family and with the knowledge of my weaknesses and strengths.

Many women have tried it and reported back that they love it. Some have felt it wasn't for them but trying it helped them work out a plan that was suitable. My working-mother neighbor tried a reverse plan. Her dinner is already arranged and only needs to be heated up when she comes home. But after dinner she putters around preparing tomorrow night's dinner, and while she does it she is completely available to her two sons who have been without her during the day.

This evening meal is much, much more than the obvious self-discipline. It is that golden opportunity that Jesus offers us in the Scriptures when He says that he who loses his life will find it (Matt. 10:39). As we adventure into the plan He has for our personal voyage, our lives will know wonderful peace as we give up what we want for what He has called us to do.

When we think of being called by God, our mind often envisions faraway mission fields. And while it can mean that, it probably won't during the years we have a family in our care. Instead, our calling most likely will be to the mundane job of dinner on time day in and day out. It becomes that great, unselfish sacrifice that enables us to lay down our lives bit by bit and follow Jesus who totally laid down His life for us. And He has promised that whenever we lose our life we find it (Matt. 10:39).

Giving of ourselves not only profits us spirtually but it becomes an offering to our family more valuable than anything we could gift wrap at Christmas. Edith Schaeffer says regarding family meals:

> Food cannot take care of spiritual, psychological and emotional problems, but the feeling of being loved and cared for, the actual comfort of the beauty and flavour of

> food, the increase of blood sugar and physical well-being,
> help one to go on during the next hours better equipped
> to meet the problems."[4]

When this is done as a gift to the Lord and the fulfilling of the calling He has placed on our lives, we know that this, too, is another way to seek first the kingdom of God. And all the good things we desire will be added unto us (Matt. 6:33).

Yet, even after dinner has been budgeted, planned, shopped for, cooked and served, one last step remains. Cleanup. My mother-in-law has a wonderful method of cleaning up as she cooks so that when she sits down to dinner all the pots and pans are put away and the counters are clean. My sister, with an efficient kitchen, doesn't seem to be bogged down by cleanup. But I've never been magician enough to master my mother-in-law's trick and for ten years we had a nightmare kitchen. I learned there was only one way to handle after-dinner cleanup — just get in there and do it. It's a final step and it must be done so that tomorrow will start fresh.

This is one of those times that it is important that we know ourselves. The *we'll-do-it-my-way-immediately* and *get-in-and-do-it-now* women who may have to get down on their knees and beg God for the grace to give time to others, will breeze right through the cleanup. However to the *I-could-care-less* type and *I'll-think-about-it-tomorrow* woman, the evening cleanup is one of the great horrors of the day. She can't do it herself and she can't make the kids do something she detests so much herself.

Dolly was such a person. She hated the dinner dishes so much that usually they were still all over the counters when she started the next night's meal. The mess of two meals was so unappealing she would take the Scarlet O'Hara approach, "I'll think about that tomorrow." If she left it long enough her husband or her embarrassed daughter would pitch in and do it for her. Dolly would feel so guilty she'd promise herself that she'd honestly do it herself from now on. But in a few days the mess would accumulate again.

At a retreat Dolly heard a speaker say that Jesus is the answer to all our problems, that we can do all things through Him who strengthens us if we will ask His help. That night, when everyone else finally settled down, she crawled out of her warm sleeping bag and knelt down on the cold cabin floor beside her bunk. Discussing her problem with Jesus she said, "Lord, I can't do it my myself; I can't clean up that kitchen every night." Then she gave the problem to Him and asked Him to be her strength and her willingness to do it.

At Dolly's house the nightly cleanup gets done now. "It's partly," she said, "because I just somehow, without even thinking about it, find myself doing it and partly because now that I'm carrying my share I can ask my daughter for her help, too."

She added, "I know something that I never understood before, the Lord's strength *is* sufficient for all things."

Each of us is called by the Lord to holiness. Isn't it amazing that so many of us answer that call through something as everyday as dinner and the dishes? The evening meal is the great paradox of our homemaker lives. It looks, at a glance, so unimportant when we consider all that there is to be done for the cause of Christ. But when we answer this calling to lay down our lives every day at 4:30 with a conscious love for the Lord, it is not only helpful beyond all understanding to those we love, but when it is done for Jesus how can it be anything but important and utterly worthwhile?

16

S&H Green Stamps

I don't know if Eloise would have labeled herself financially well-off, but from my point of view that seemed to sum up the situation. She had enough money to go anywhere, do anything and buy anything she wanted without asking the price. One of the fun aspects of knowing her was her wonderful sense of abandon regarding money. Often she made an extravagant purchase which she gave away the next day to some casual acquaintance who might express delight in it.

To me the most curious aspect of Eloise was not that she gave away the purchases, but that she even bothered to save the S & H Green Stamps that came along with them. We don't get stamps in Washington, but in Oregon where Eloise lived, green stamps are given with every purchase. It takes zillions, it seems, to fill a book, but a book or several books can be traded for a wonderful assortment of prizes.

Almost dutifully, Eloise rescued stamps from the bottom of her shopping bags and stuck them in a little book as soon as she returned home. "Why, Eloise? Why bother?" I asked her, "You don't need them; you'll probably turn your book of stamps in on a prize that you'll give away before you get home."

"And why not?" she boomed. "Why waste anything just because you've got a lot of it?" Then she added in a slightly softer way, "Besides, I can't throw them away. I tried that before when I've been in a hurry and it makes me feel, well, it's hard to say, but like someone is offering me something and it just doesn't seem right to turn it down."

"I understand," I told her. "That's exactly the way I feel about time. God has given it to us, and although we may have plenty of it, it's a shame to throw out even a little bit." We discussed how a relatively few stamps can redeem something useful. A set of dishes can be earned piece by piece. There are toys for Christmas and useful gadgets for Father's Day to be earned with the stamps that just might be thrown in the glove compartment.

The parallel with time is obvious. Just as Eloise made use of her S & H green stamps instead of wasting them, spare minutes and hours can be useful tools, too. A college professor once told a graduating class, "I hope that when you are all married and your wife tells you she is almost ready to go with you except for a couple of last-minute touches, you will sit down with a book and read. You will be surprised at how much knowledge you will acquire." Dick Schneider, a *Guideposts Magazine* editor, apparently in agreement with this, insists that he read the whole Great Books library just during the accumulative time that he waited for his wife Betty to get ready.

Someone has said that in just ten minutes of Bible reading a day, you could read the whole Bible in a year. Two years ago I tried it and found that this is true.

It is safe to say that in a period of a lifetime one probably spends at least one full year of just waiting. So it's good to plan to use the minutes we spend in that waiting time to our advantage.

Waiting on the phone is a good time to pray for the person we are calling. Bill uses the pause at red lights when he is driving as additional prayer time for the family. I have a wonderful mother-in-law who, if she has a moment to spare, cleans one shelf of a cupboard. The best part is that she does it at my house.

Bill Jr.'s wife Mari is a natural artist. Her Indian heritage has blessed her with ability in nearly every art form incuding turning a piece of hide into beaded moccasins, but the arrival of baby Chariti changed all that. There were no more large blocks of time for creative work and Mari found herself growing frustrated with the work of a baby and the lack of time.

Then she decided that art work didn't need a special time slot. Instead, she began to use the little snatches of time, the moments when Chariti was being good, to work on her projects. And so the beautiful art of which we are often recipients continues on and Mari is content for now.

Often we can use the time when our minds are busy to work with our hands.

I often jot down all the little jobs that can be done while I'm on the telephone. When someone wants to talk, I get out the toothbrush and scrub the tile in the kitchen (4,121 tiles) or clean the stove top or wash the canisters. When the phone call is over, so is one more little job in the kitchen.

We can also do just the opposite and use our physical working time for some mental work as well.

"Keep praying earnestly for all Christians everywhere," Paul urged the Ephesians (Eph. 6:18 TLB). A young housewife who is doing exactly that is Judy Molitor. Judy has been prayerfully concerned for the government during the last two years. Although busy with four children, dozens of interests and a sixteen-room house, she has been able to keep the cause of good government in constant prayer. She says she sings in tongues for the president and our lawmakers as she pushes the vacuum over her many carpeted floors. Making beds reminds her to pray for one person, going up and down the stairs reminds her of still another.

While eighteen-year-old Anne scrubbed tables in the college cafeteria, her mind was busy in a special prayer. "Dear Lord, please, please don't let Mary Lou get an abortion. Lord, You know she'll always be sorry. Help her not to be afraid and help her to tell her mom. Please, please help her." And with every "please" she scrubbed harder until all twenty-seven tables were gleaming and the problems of Mary Lou were thoroughly presented to the Lord.

Driving somewhere with a child can be an opportunity to use a good-sized piece of time for one-to-one communication. When our children were all at home, it was always challenging to give them enough personal time. Often I would say, "Paul, (or Katy, or John,) do you want to come to the store with me?" Sometimes when I drove with the child he shared experiences he would never have had time to share in their entirety at home.

Once Bill had to drive several teen-agers to a ferry dock that was two hours away and four-year-old Joe went along for the ride. As soon as the big kids were out of the car Joe, our quiet little Joe, began to talk. He talked and talked and talked for the entire two-hour drive home as Bill realized for the first time how much our little fellow had to say and how little chance he had to say it.

Riding can also be a time to communicate with the Lord. Mary Mauren, a Seattle prayer group leader, tells of the time when she was driving alone and heard her name called out loud, "Mary!" There was no one in the car and yet she knew she had not imagined it.

Then she remembered an earlier conversation with a friend. "I've grown so far away from God He doesn't even know my name," she'd said.

But there on the highway just before the fire station she knew with a certainty that He had not forgotten her, but indeed He had called her by name. Thus began some wonderful in-car prayer dialogues with Him. As Mary's own world changed, the worlds of hundreds of others in her community changed also as they have come in touch with Mary's vibrant faith in prayer.

Sometimes we find a spot of time unexpectedly. When Kitty Silvernale (twelve children still at home) found that her youngest child, Keough, was not progressing socially, she took her to nursery school. But instead of gaining that time for herself, Kitty found that she had given up the morning, in fact several a week, for Keough needed her to stay close by. So Kitty sat on a chair where Keough could see her when she needed reassuring and inwardly moaned about the waste of time. There was so much to be done at home!

After a week it occurred to Kitty that the door to extra time had been opened for her instead of banged shut as it had looked at first glance. She began to bring with her all the things there hadn't been time for in the past 18 years: letters she had always intended to write, autobiographies, and histories she had only half-read and luxury of luxuries, the embroidered pillowcases she had begun when her oldest child was still a baby. The mornings for Keough became also mornings for Kitty.

Sometimes we can turn a wasted piece of time into recreation. Whenever Bill would call and say he'd be an hour late, I was inwardly irritated at this waste of time. (Actually I would storm around quite a bit.) It seemed to me that his lateness added a superfluous hour to the afternoon and subtracted it from the busy evening. I felt this way until I decided to use the time for something unrelated to either before or after dinner. There is a path behind our back door that leads to the shores of Puget Sound. It is surprising how seldom I use it to walk to the beach and just enjoy sitting on the sand. But it occurred to me one day that this perhaps was a perfect way to use that additional hour. Now when Bill is delayed, the little children and I tramp down the path. They play by the shore while I sit there and listen to the water and gulls and rejoice in the moments the Lord has provided. A much better pastime than waiting furiously at home!

Jesus made the most of every opportunity. While He waited for His disciples to bring food, He began a conversation with a Samaritan woman. The results were that many people in that "second cousin" city of Samaria began to believe that Jesus was indeed the Messiah. As Jesus walked from village to village with His disciples He used the time to teach much of what they would have to know. Jesus knew how to use His time so well that when He crossed the Sea of Galilee with His disciples He caught up on His rest by falling asleep in the hull of the boat.

In every life there comes a time when there are large unspoken-for blocks of time. Just as we can make wonderful purchases with shopping bags full of green stamps, those who have shopping bags of time can also turn them into something of great value to the Christian community.

Invalids have this time, especially time for prayer. At a seminar I heard of a pastor who knew very well how much his work needed an undergirding of prayer. He went to all the infirm people in his church and begged their prayers for the good of the parish. He reported, "With that harnessed prayer everything changed for the better. People who had fallen away came back. Women who hadn't talked to each other for years became friends, strangers came to the rectory and accepted Jesus as their Savior."

Many people who spend an endless wilderness of time in bed have prayerfully taken on the needs of the pastor and those around them. Others, in addition, have even concerned themselves with the physical and emotional well-being of another person. Such an experience was shared by Catherine Marshall. During the time in her life when she suffered from tuberculosis, Catherine spent her days in an upstairs bedroom. She had done all she could to make the passage of time less agonizing. But even with a schedule of prayer and devotions, reading, meals, researching for Peter Marshall's sermons, games and books with her son Peter John, there was still some time left over.

Then she and her housekeeper put their heads together on an exciting plan. There was a young woman in her church who was deeply discouraged; her attitude and appearance was one of "I'm not worth bothering with." Catherine and her housekeeper decided to launch a series of notes and gifts and leave them anonymously on her doorstep.

How surprised this young woman must have been to arrive home from work and find a little present wrapped for her on the front stoop. In it was a card that said other gifts would be coming from time to time. Catherine and her housekeeper sent a book, a cake, a basket of hot rolls, a pretty handkerchief, and the caring made a noticeable change in the young woman's life. She was given such a lift that even her outward appearance began to look different. The impression of self-confidence transformed her face and walk until all who knew her noticed.

Besides the infirm, the retired also have large blocks of time to give. My father, who had a dozen projects lined up for his retirement, grew quite concerned about Mother's time because she didn't have a hobby like he did. She didn't garden or tinker in a workshop or enjoy the greenhouse. She didn't care for television or puzzles and Dad grew worried that she was going to be a problem to him when they retired. In preparation he bought her a sewing machine with five free lessons and an organ with five free lessons. He promised her that if she would just learn to knit or crochet he would pay for all the yarn.

Really, Mother tried. She made an apron and a nightgown for our Katy on the sewing machine and even covered a lawn swing to prove to herself that she could do it, but sewing just wasn't her interest. She took organ lessons and learned to play *She'll Be Coming Round the Mountain* and *Silent Night,* but that was enough of that, too. She learned to crochet but that wasn't her portion, either.

What Dad hadn't counted on was the hobby Mother had always had through the years, the hobby of people. Retirement to Mom means teaching in the Frank Laubach literary course, the each-one-teach-one program. It means starting a Bible study for lonely older women; it means collecting blankets for missions; it means special days with our Katy or Danny, who think Grandma is wonderful; it means helping a blind lady and keeping contact with old friends; it means time and prayer for her children and grandchildren. ("Hello, Mom, would you pray about this?")

In no way does Mother's retirement resemble a shopping

bag with green stamps tossed in the corner. She has taken her great commodity of time and returned the investment to the lives of those around her.

John Howe once said, "What folly, to dread the thought of throwing away life at once, and yet have no regard to throwing it away by parcel and piecemeal." Another way to say it comes from the Living Bible: "So be careful how you act; these are difficult days. Don't be fools; be wise: make the most of every opportunity you have for doing good. Don't act thoughtlessly, but try to find out and do whatever the Lord wants you to" (Eph. 5:15-17).

We can redeem the minutes and hours in our lives as we would redeem the stamps of a book, not ungratefully wasting the gift that has been given to us, but using it to its greatest advantage.

17

My Time, is His Time,

The most delightful fact of all regarding time is simply this: the creator of time is also the giver of time. When we have exhausted our supply, used up our twenty-four hours, and still need time, an amazing thing can happen to those who ask for it. God will give us time. I don't know how it happens, but many people besides myself have experienced it. God can do this for one reason—time belongs to Him.

Who can explain God's ownership of our time better than C. S. Lewis who writes of it in his delightful book *The Screwtape Letters*? The book is a series of letters supposedly from an experienced demon named Screwtape to his young demon nephew, Wormwood, schooling him in the art of tempting men away from God.

The older demon writes: "You must . . . zealously guard

in his [man's] mind the curious assumption, 'My time is my own . . .'

"You have here a delicate task. The assumption which you want him to go on making is so absurd that, if once it is questioned, even we cannot find a shred of argument in its defense. The man can neither make, nor retain, one moment of time; it all comes to him by pure gift; he might as well regard the sun and moon as his chattels.'"[1]

No, time is not our own. Just as we belong to the Father, so also does our time. If we can understand this it will give new meaning to our search. For if we will walk in union with Jesus we can ask the Father for anything in His name and He will give it to us (John 14:14).

I had the privilege of discussing with Catherine Marshall how God is the giver of time. "Have you ever had the experience of asking God to give you His love for someone you couldn't love yourself?" she asked.

I nodded, remembering Sonny, an "impossible" neighbor boy who destroyed trikes and wagons and daily made all the children cry. Desperately, I prayed, "Father, I cannot love him, but I know You love him. Please give me Your love for him."

I can't explain how it happpened, but that very day as he began his destructive ways, I found myself going out into the backyard and saying, "Sonny, come in. I want to talk to you." There was no anger, just sort of a loving feeling for him I'd never known before.

I brought him in, thinking I'd talk to him about the toys he had broken, but instead I said, "Have a cookie." He stuffed one into his mouth, then another and another. "Sonny, are you awfully hungry?"

"Uh huh."

So we made a deal. Anytime he wanted to, he could come in and make a peanut butter and jelly sandwich, but he must help me take care of the children when they were outside.

The evening with Catherine wasn't long enough to share this story, so I just acknowledged I had experienced God's giving me His love when I had had none of my own.

"Then," she said, "if we can ask Him for love that is not ours, I believe we can ask Him for time that is not ours."

Because I believed it, too, I asked the Lord to send others across my path who had experienced it in their lives. A short while later Nora Tilton, a woman who had heard of my interest in time, called to share her experience.

One morning, during her sixth pregnancy, when she was feeling worn out before the day had even begun, she had prayed, "Lord, I need to do all the laundry, drive three car pools, make the grapes into juice, and do the beds, kitchen, and meals. Please help me." She was barely back from driving the first car pool when a friend called who needed her full attention. Nora had no sooner hung up from a long telephone chat with her and started her work when another friend knocked at the door. "Am I bothering you? I need to talk to someone." Nora put her work aside again. When the friend left, Nora drove the kindergarten car pool and returned home. As she was throwing some laundry into the machine, another friend in need called on the phone.

Nora was not frustrated. "I had asked the Lord to help me find the time," she said, "and I knew He would." As soon as she hung up from distraction number three, Nora somehow made the beds, finished up the laundry, made the grape juice, began dinner, and finished in time to drive the third car pool. "I don't know how it happened—I did not have enough time to get all that work done. But when I ask the Lord for time, He always gives it to me."

Another experience came through the mail in a letter from John Sherill, the author of *They Speak in Other Tongues:*[2]

> I made a discovery some years ago about the task of preparing my income tax. I put the whole process into a framework of prayer. "Lord, You know that this is a segment of time which I must set aside for this purpose. Since I must do this, I am simply going to wait until You prepare the time for me." Then I put my income tax papers out on the table. I did this about a month ahead of deadline and I simply waited. Every day I took a look at

the papers with no anxiety that I wasn't going to get them done on time. I went about my regular routine without feeling frustrations and conflicts for the use of time. I had a confidence that, since the Lord knew of this need, He would supply.

And that's exactly what did happen. One day an appointment that would have taken a huge chunk of time was cancelled. I knew instantly that this was the Lord's time for my tax. I turned to it with a great sense of continuing relaxation about the time requirement, knowing that if I didn't get through it now, there would be more time available. But most important of all, I thoroughly enjoyed preparing my income tax. It allowed me an opportunity to review nostalgically all the interesting and good things that had happened to Tib and me over the year as they reflected in the travel chits, entertainment, etc. Since then I have always found that this dreaded expense of time will yield to this technique.

Another young woman came to the house and asked if I would like to hear her little story about God giving her time. Pat Hogan has three preschool children who seem to need her constant attention. One of the great satisfactions of her life is her Bible study class, but Pat grinned and said:

Three little children and daily time for Bible study are incompatible. At least they were until I prayed a rather curious prayer. Twice a week I needed to sit down at 10:00 and study for forty-five minutes. Always it seemed that that was the time when bedlam grew worse and the phone rang and rang. Then one morning I prayed, "Jesus, please keep this next forty-five minutes protected from interruption."

I settled the children with something to do and began the lesson. The children played without a quarrel. The house was quiet, no one came or called and I was able to get all my studying done. At the end of the forty-five minutes the phone rang, the children began quarreling and needing some attention. I said, "Oh, thank You, Lord, for that protected time." Then I began to wonder if it was a coincidence. But since then it has happened over and over, enough to show me that *Jesus truly is the Lord of our time.*

Gretchen Earley tells another story of a day when she trusted time-to-get-everything-done to the Lord:

> It was Sunday morning and due to unexpected activities on Saturday, my house was a perfect mess. I had invited my parents for dinner for their wedding anniversary and, although they had to drive a great distance, they were well-known for always arriving an hour before the appointed time.
>
> In my mind I outlined what had to be done to the house as well as meal preparation and I felt the not-enough-time panic closing in. There was an alternative; I could skip church. Then I remembered our weekly Bible study class which was stressing our yieldedness to the Spirit and to His lordship over everything, even time. So I said, "Lord, if I go to Your house this morning and yield my hours to You, somehow You will have to make enough time for me to get all these things accomplished. Thank You, Father." I asked my husband to pray about it also but didn't mention it to my two teen-agers who were staying home due to colds.
>
> By the time I arrived home from church a slight bit of apprehension was growing again but to my amazement and joy the house was clean. The children had decided it needed straightening and had pitched in together. My heart overflowed with this unexpected answer to prayer. As a bonus blessing, for the very first time my parents were one-half hour late.

There came a day in my own life when I wondered if maybe I could be wrong about the Lord being the giver of the time we need. My prayer that morning had included the specific request for time during the next two days to write and finish an important article for *Aglow Magazine.* Just as I finished the prayer the phone rang. It was Tricia, a woman in our prayer community who runs a communal hospitality house for temporarily homeless people. "Pat, the baby of a transient family who is staying here, died last night. Can you take the other six children in the household for me today?"

Even as I was saying I could, I wondered how the Lord was going to give me enough time to finish that article, but I was certain He would. My friend, Virginia, came over and together we made it through the morning with eight preschoolers, and I presumed that while the children rested the Lord would give my writing wings. I settled four of the children in the upstairs bedroom and began to settle the rest in the front room. "Now, you two boys, take this davenport and you two girls, take . . . oh oh, where's Monique?" The three I had just settled got up and we searched the bedrooms, bathrooms and closets, calling her name, looking for her mop of red hair. "Where could a two-year-old go?" I asked.

"She runs away sometimes," one of the children answered.

Good grief, had she taken the path to the beach or the dangerous road where all the accidents occur? I sent the five-year-olds to the beach with a strong directive not to go into the water, put a four-year-old girl in charge of the little ones while I checked with the neighbors. The neighbors hadn't seen her; the boys came back without her. I called the sheriff and described her. His office said they would check the beach first. Where had she gone? Her family had lost one baby this very day; they couldn't lose another one. I jumped into the car and went down the dangerous road. Half a mile away I saw a head of frizzy red curls. She was walking along the street holding a man's hand. I rolled down the window. "Monique!"

The man brought her to me, great relief on his face. He had found her heading for the water, rescued her and had been asking everyone if they knew her. I thanked him (I hope I did, the lump in my throat was almost too big to say anything) and put her in the car. At home I called the sheriff, settled everyone again, and sat down to my desk. Ten minutes later the school children walked in the door. The day was over and the time to write was completely gone. And I did really wonder why. I knew that I had everything in right order, I knew I could ask for enough time and expect that the Lord would provide it. Now there wasn't enough time and I felt puzzled.

The next morning before the breakfast dishes were even started, a friend called inviting my two boys on an all-day outing. They left at 9 a.m. with their lunches packed in brown bags (like the big kids) and with a whole morning I hadn't counted on, I wrote the two-day article in one day.

Yes, God is the Lord of our time. He does give us time to do the things we need to do. My friend, Virginia, is a woman who walks with the Lord and knows His ways. She insists that God is such a force in the lives of people who will trust Him that He plans their day, including *not* providing time for the things He does not want them to do. "He delays us, puts us in unusual places we couldn't have planned for and changes our path. When something comes up to take our time from a previously planned project, we don't have to feel frustrated because He is in charge of our moments just as surely as He is in control of the universe."

A Bible Study Fellowship teacher, Winnie Dong, told of a time she and her minister husband were driving to an important pastors' convention in Canada when car trouble in a remote little town held them up for several hours while parts were being located. Winnie and her husband were totally at peace, knowing that since their time was the Lord's, He had allowed this particular delay to happen for a reason. They sat so unconcerned in their car that the service station owner finally couldn't stand it. He peered in the window and demanded to know, "What's with you people? How can you be so patient? Anyone else would be furious."

"We're Christians," Pastor Dong said, "and we believe that we can trust the Lord in every circumstance." For the next few hours, while they waited for the parts to arrive, Winnie and her husband shared the wonderful truths of salvation with this man who had never heard them before.

They didn't make it to the pastors' convention, but instead

turned around for home, praising God the rest of their journey for the young man who had accepted Jesus as his Savior.

Sometimes Jesus has something planned for our time that we don't want to do at all. My friend, Charlotte, looked forward all week to Sunday afternoon when her husband took their four active children on an outing and left her at home to have some time for herself. She was always especially relieved to get away from her ever-active ten-year-old Larry, who had been unexplainably irritable and rebellious lately. But one Sunday Larry threw a rock at a neighbor's cat and broke a window as well as one of Charlotte's rules. As a punishment, Charlotte told him that this Sunday he could positively not go with his father. No treats for him when he was disobedient.

But as two o'clock came and Larry grew more and more obnoxious, everything in her wanted to get him out of the house for a few hours so she could just rest. She went into her bedroom to pray. "Jesus, You know I need some time with myself. Would it be all right to let him go?"

The answer came back almost before she had finished asking. "No, he needs you to follow through on your punishment."

As Larry balked and pouted, Charlotte remained firm. Hoping to interest him in a pastime, she laid out a game on the table. He was too irritated with her to even talk and went out to sit on the back steps. Still Charlotte hoped she could take a nap. She also wished the Lord would do something to this boy to change him but that seemed impossible. Then Larry came back in and said defiantly, "I'll play the stupid game if you'll play it too."

Larry waited for her answer; Charlotte knew the Lord was asking her to give up "her" special Sunday time. As Charlotte and Larry played the game, the communication that had been closed for weeks opened between them. Larry explained about the rock-throwing incident, apologized for his behavior and admitted that he would have been disappointed if she had let him go.

Charlotte did not get a nap or her time alone that week, but she went to bed that night far more rested from the breakthrough with Larry. She commented to me many years later, "I've found that when we acknowledge our time is the Lord's we give it away. When He gives it back it is not always in the form we think it should be, yet it is always right for us."

In the same way experience has shown Bill and me that we can always trust that Jesus, whom we've made Lord of our time, will not let us down. Last fall, Paul, one of our teenagers asked, "If I take care of everything after dinner, could you and Dad drive to the Northgate Shopping Center by 7 p.m. because there is a good sale on tennis shoes and a free basketball for the first 250 people to come?"

We agreed to do it, partly because Paul asks so few favors and partly because we had to be close to the center at 9:30 that night. We dashed out of the house and got to Northgate just at 7 p.m. that night, and amazingly in view of such a grand sale, had no trouble getting a parking spot. We hurried into the store and found that we had come on the wrong night.

After a moment's shock it dawned on us both that there must be a reason for it. We sat in the car and asked, "What is it, Lord? What are we supposed to do? Who are we supposed to see?" We were both positive God wouldn't let us waste two and one-half hours. I thought of our daughter-in-law Annette who lived close by and she was the person who came to Bill's mind, too.

When we arrived at Annette's we found her alone with the baby. I don't even know how the conversation started, but within five minutes of our arrival she began sharing how for two weeks she had doubted the worth of Christianity and the reality of God. Bill shared for an hour as she asked question after question. Then we prayed with her and counseled her about the snares of the enemy. Over and over she thanked us for coming. We left for our commitment rejoicing, knowing that we can count on the Lord to use the time He has given us to His best advantage.

The Lord did not let Paul down, either. The next night

Annette and Dave went to Northgate and bought Paul's tennis shoes and even managed to get him a free basketball.

We can expect this kind of guidance just as Jesus expected the guidance of the Father as He walked this earth. *He was always in the right spot at the right time.* He was in Capernaum just when the centurion's son became ill. He was in Nain just as the widow's son's funeral was passing and the crowds came to Him for healing. The Father had given Him a message to teach but He didn't have to search for people to listen. They sought Him out. He did not apologize for not curing or teaching the crowds while His physical body was being restored and refreshed. Jesus flowed with the hours of the day. He always had enough time.

So it can be for us.

18

Setting
Sail

In order to sail into the adventure the Lord has planned for us, we need the Holy Spirit to blow through our lives each day to set us in motion. Eadie Goodboy, from the Aglow Publications staff tells how she takes everything that must be done in the day and using the kitchen table as an altar, lays it out before the Lord. Then she asks the Holy Spirit to lead her through each moment and help her accomplish every task ahead in His perfect timing.

Christian leaders of every denomination it seems, agree that putting the day in the hands of the Lord and letting His Holy Spirit work is the most victorious way to begin each morning. In particular, I was impressed with the way one of the volunteer workers at the magazine office, Marietta Oswald, begins her day.

Marietta is not a famous person, just an ordinary Christian wife, mother, grandma and Penney's shoe department clerk. There is a peace about her that everyone notices; it's in her face, her talk, her actions. One senses that she knows Jesus well. Her way of flowing with the hours of the day as Jesus did can be ours as well. Marietta begins her day with a prayer she calls her *morning offering:*

Dear Jesus, I offer to You this day and ask the Holy Spirit to guide my ways at all times. I ask that time will be used efficiently, that I will not be so rushed I cannot smile, that I will be Your tool, that I will meet people I should meet, that I will share Your love. I ask that as I use Your time, You will give me time to accomplish everything on my list today.

"This prayer," she said, "this offering of time to the Lord, this expectation of the Holy Spirit's guidance takes a minute in the morning and it sets the day in motion. Once it is prayed, everything seems to fall in place."

I asked the Lord to send me the right people, ordinary Christian women who have offered their day to Jesus, and who let the Holy Spirit blow through their lives. Once again people began calling, or stopping by or sending notes about what had happened to them. Let's think about their experiences in the words of Marietta's morning prayer:

That time will be used efficiently. Bev Chamberlain, one of my generous typists, had to take her teen-age daughter Caryn shopping for a pattern, coat and lining material. Caryn, like most teen-agers, finds decisions are hard to make, so shopping with her has always been a long, time-consuming ordeal for Bev. Also, as a working mother, Bev needs to be home with her other children as much as possible in the evenings. She also must do her housework at night as well as call customers on the phone. In addition, the evening they had picked for shopping was the night of Caryn's Bible class, something she regularly looked for an excuse to get out of going to.

Bev, seeing what was ahead of her that day, knew she couldn't handle it. But she knew Jesus could. Her *morning offering* included a specific prayer that each item that was ahead of her would work out efficiently.

In the very first store, Caryn found a pattern that she liked immediately. A sales clerk just happened to remember three $20-a-yard camel colored remnants on sale for $4.50 a yard. Caryn liked them at once. At another fabric store, they found a maroon and tan plaid that Caryn pronounced perfect for the lining. As they walked outside, their bus came within a minute. The family had dinner ready, and afterward Caryn went off to the Bible study class "reluctantly," Bev said, "but at least she went." Bev cleaned a drawer, read the children a Bible story, put them to bed and called customers on the phone for an hour. Every customer was available, and when she hung up from the last call, Caryn came home "absolutely exuberant." In telling this to me, Bev emphasized that she is not efficient. But the Holy Spirit is.

That I will not be so rushed I cannot smile. Barbara, a reading consultant at school, is another working mom who prayed for help. Unlike Bev, who had specific things ahead of her to be done, Barbara had so much ahead of her, she didn't know where to start. Usually she and the three children sat around in the afternoon, the house so messy Barb was miserable. "My husband was such a grouch," she said, "it was no incentive to clean up for him." Then one day everything changed. Barbara offered her home day (working moms have two days, the one that starts with their job and the other one that starts when they get home) to the Lord and asked the Holy Spirit to guide her.

At once she was impressed to begin picking up all the clutter. As long as she was working on the house, she felt it was all right to ask for the children's help. Then she was impressed to bake a cake.

When her husband came home and saw his household in order and smelled the cake, he wasn't grouchy at all. He was so happy that she and the children felt happy. Sexually the couple had been far apart, but that night she welcomed his affections. After a month of committing her time to Jesus and asking what He wanted her to do, Barbara bubbled over as she spoke on the phone. "I'm so happy with myself and, what's more exciting, the change in me has made Bob want to become a Christian."

That I will be Your tool. A grandmotherly woman whose *morning offering* always includes the desire to be God's tool is Genevieve Miller. She wrote me the following letter recently from the resort fishing town where she lives year around.

> We had such an experience the other night. Walter and I were sitting here alone when the doorbell rang. I opened the door and a woman nearly fell on top of me. "Are you sick?" I asked and she nodded. I brought her in and she *was* sick, drunk and sick. She, her husband and a friend had been downtown drinking; she had fought with her husband and started walking. She said she didn't know why she had knocked at our door, but I'm certain it was because I had promised to earnestly pray each morning to be used by the Lord.
>
> She gave me a friend's name in a little trailer town where she lives, 65 miles out in the country. I called, but no one was there. Walter and I told her not to worry, but to stay until we could locate a friend to help her.
>
> Soon she started telling me her life story. She felt that God thought she was too unimportant for Him. I hugged her and assured her differently, telling her of His great love and how she could accept Jesus as her Savior by just asking Him to forgive her sins and come into her heart.
>
> At last we located her friend and, as she left, I gave her the name of a devout girl in her trailer town who, herself, had seen the seamy side of life. As she left, she took my hand and held it for a moment. "No one has ever made me feel so good and clean and full of hope." My prayers go with her. It was an exciting evening.

That I will meet people I should meet. Joyce Foss' problem was the loneliness that came from too much time on her hands. One day she asked the Holy Spirit, "What does Jesus want me to do?" She said, "No sooner had I asked this when He began sending me friends, not just ordinary ones but those who needed a friend, all handicapped in a physical or emotional way." Joyce began sharing her life and possessions and the new friends became friends with each other. "Now I have much to do," she said. "The people He has sent me have taken away the loneliness and I am filled with His peace instead."

That I will share Your love. Loving was hard for Nancy McLaughlin when her Dad came to live with her. She said:

> We had never been close, never affectionate or open in our feelings with one another. Over the years the Lord had shown me many resentments I had toward Dad that He wanted to touch. I felt this time when Dad came I would really attempt to put things right, let Jesus live through me in such a way that even Dad would see a difference. To some degree this happened. He could see a difference in my life but I also found my old resentments and hostilities coming back through things he did which annoyed me.
>
> It came to a culmination when I walked into the pantry and discovered that Dad had spilled quite a bit of sugar. Dad, trying to clean it up himself, had used an almost-full vacuum bag which had finally rejected the sugar. Sugar was everywhere . . . in the bag, on the floor and in the parts of the machine itself. I wanted to scream. Instead, I went to work cleaning out that gummy vacuum cleaner. I was seething inside and it took a fair amount of time to get the job done, just enough time for the Holy Spirit to show what He was doing in my life.   There was enough time for me to ask forgiveness and experience a peace and love concerning my father that I hadn't known before. By the time the vacuum was clean and shiny again, I was able to go to my dad and ask his forgiveness. I also added that I loved him. To my amazement his eyes filled with tears and for the first time we were able to speak to one another from our hearts. A healing work of God was begun in our lives.

That . . . You will give me time to accomplish everything on my list today. For many years I offered not only my day but each little thing I wanted to accomplish to Jesus and asked Him to let His Holy Spirit show me the time to do it. Whenever anyone asked, "How do you manage?" I would answer, "It's the Holy Spirit."

Then one evening at a Christmas party, a woman who is a Christian by anybody's standards, exclaimed when I gave her my answer, "Well, I have the Holy Spirit, too, and I'm not accomplishing a thing compared to you."

I went home and let her words race around in my mind

like a two-year-old in a department store. Shambles resulted. It wasn't too long before I began telling myself, "I'm naturally well-organized. I have a flair for managing well." Gradually, I became convinced that it was I who kept things going as smoothly as possible; it wasn't the Holy Spirit after all.

For awhile I was able to run on my own steam. But it wasn't too long after I began trusting in myself alone that I wasn't able to get to my desk each day. I said, "Well, I'm almost forty."

I don't know how long this would have gone on but during the first week of June an old writing friend, Jean, stopped by to see what I was doing in the writing field. On my desk, instead of something productive, was yesterday's laundry. When she asked to use the bathroom I was embarrassed at the terrible mess I knew she was going to find.

After she left I ran around and tried to do up some of the undone work. I knew I was locking the barn door after the horse had been stolen but I was so embarrassed I didn't know what else to do.

That night I awoke about two and crawled out of bed. The street light gave just enough light to keep me from tripping over the toys on the front room floor. Down on my knees in the shadowed darkness I prayed, "Jesus, it *is* Your Holy Spirit, isn't it? It is He who helps me plan and make lists and get the work done, isn't it? When I offered my day to You, You did help me take care of the family and the house and the writing. I'm sorry. I've been so foolish. Why did I ever think I was doing it myself?"

I did something then that I hadn't done since that Christmas party. I talked to Him about everything on my list and asked His Holy Spirit to help me do it. "In the morning I need to organize the children's work, shop, clean the bathrooms, clear off my desk and bake a cake. I don't know how I'll do it with the baby still needing so much attention but I know with my day in Your hands it can be done."

It was. When Bill came home from work and saw the house in order and a cake made he exclaimed, "How did you do it?''

I told him that it was the Holy Spirit.

The *morning offering,* putting the Holy Spirit in charge of each day, is the final task we have in completing the puzzle, for it gently links each section together. With each piece in place, the picture is as stunning as we knew it would be. Above and behind we've placed the soft blue and white pieces of the sky, the purposes, goals, priorities and plans, in a way that is just right for us. Beneath us are the deeply colored aquamarine pieces, the right order in our lives, that we need for sailing: prayer on top; our husbands, second; our children and family, third; our community outreach stretching across the bottom. Behind us are the rich brown greens of land joining with the water and sky to give us the supportive planning we need to get under way.

There we are in the center, each different in our own picture just as the land, sky and water in each picture is completely varied. Each of us is beautiful as we sail with confidence, letting the Holy Spirit blow us along the course Jesus has mapped out for us. We can trust, wholly, that when we have done our share, God who is the creator of time will give us all the time we need for the great adventure of doing all He has called us to do.

EPILOGUE

Did you wonder as you read this book where all the stories of women's confrontations with time came from? Almost entirely, they came from women like yourselves. I spoke to several hundred women in groups and individually and asked them to share their stories of time in their lives. And they did. They came for a cup of tea, or called on the phone if they were in town, or wrote a letter. Now I wonder if you will do the same? If you have a story about time you'd like to share I'd love to hear from you.

One more aspect of time to consider is the tithe of our time. We've heard the wonderful things that happen to the finances of Christians when they tithe (give 10 percent of their income to the Lord). It's been suggested that we can also tithe our time. I've never done it consciously or known any woman who has, yet there must be great blessing attached to it. It would be exciting to hear from readers who have done it. How would it work? Do we tithe our waking time or the whole twenty-four hours (net or gross)? Would we give the whole tithe to others or would we spend part or all in prayer? Would it be better to tithe three days a month?

I think there are possibilities here that are undreamed of. Do you tithe your time or do you want to try it? Either way, would you share what is happening in your life? I know that I, as well as readers of subsequent books, would be blessed by hearing from you.

My address is:

Pat King
Aglow Publications
Dept. #10
7715 - 236th S.W.
Edmonds, WA 98020

Barbara's planner entitled *That Reminds Me* may be purchased at your local bookstore or ordered from:

Aglow Publications
7715 - 236th S.W.
Edmonds, WA 98020

The cost for the one-year planner is $1.50.

Notes

Chapter 2 — The Not-So-Catchy Slogan

1. Corrie ten Boom, *The Hiding Place* (Washington Depot, Connecticut: Chosen Books, 1971), pp. 192, 213.

Chapter 4 — First Things First

1. Irene B. Harrell, *Prayerables* (Waco, Texas: Word Books, 1967), p. 19.

2. Catherine Marshall, *Something More* (Carmel, New York: Guidepost Associates, 1974), pp. 35-57.

Chapter 5 — Something Worthwhile

1. Hannah Whitall Smith, *The Christian's Secret of a Happy Life* (Old Tappan, New Jersey: Fleming H. Revell Company, 1968), p. 137.

Chapter 6 — The Miserable Years

1. James Dobson, *Hide or Seek* (Old Tappan, New Jersey: Fleming H. Revell Company, 1974), p. 54.

Chapter 8 — Getting to Know Me

1. Brother Andrew, *God's Smuggler* (New York, N.Y.: The New American Library, Inc., 1967).

2. Dr. William Nolen, *McCall's Magazine* (New York, N.Y., February, 1973), p. 12.

Chapter 9 — Make It a Game

1. Ted W. Engstrom and R. Alec Mackenzie, *Managing Your Time* (Grand Rapids, Michigan: Zondervan Books, 1967), p. 53 (used by permission).

Chapter 10 — Barbara's Planner

1. Barbara's planner, *That Reminds Me,* may be ordered as specified on page 170.

Chapter 12 — The Urgent vs. the Important

1. Mary Lagrand Bouma, *The Creative Homemaker* (Minneapolis, Minnesota: Bethany Fellowship, Inc., 1973), p. 37.

2. Alan Lakein, *How to Get Control of Your Time and Your Life* (New York, N.Y.: Peter H. Wyden, Inc., 1973), pp. 87, 89.

3. James T. McCay, *The Management of Time* (Englewood Cliffs, New Jersey: Prentice-Hall, Inc.).

4. The worksheet is from the World Vision MARC Management Series, Missions Advanced Research & Communication Center, 919 West Huntington Beach, Monrovia, California 91016.

Chapter 13 — Time Off for the Cook

1. Charlie W. Shedd, *Time for All Things* (Nashville, Tennessee: Abingdon Press, 1962).

2. Marabel Morgan, *The Total Woman* (Old Tappan, New Jersey: Fleming H. Revell Company, 1973), p. 93.

Chapter 14 — Why Not Let George Do It?

1. Alec R. Mackenzie, *The Time Trap* (New York, N.Y.: American Management Association, Inc.), p. 135.

2. Ibid.

3. Ibid.

4. Ibid.

Chapter 15 — How to Beat the Four-Thirty Syndrome

1. For recipes using soybean meat substitute, send a self-addressed envelope to Pat King, Aglow Publications, Dept. 10, 7715 - 236th S.W., Edmonds, WA 98020.

2. Boyce Rensberger, *The Reader's Digest* (Pleasantville, N.Y.: The Reader's Digest Assoc., March, 1975), p. 198, condensed from *The New York Times*.

3. The money saved in using soybeans may be sent to World Vision, Box O, Pasadena, CA 91109.

4. Edith Schaeffer, *Hidden Art* (London, England: Norfolk Press, 1971), p. 124.

Chapter 17 — My Time is His Time

1. C.S. Lewis, *The Screwtape Letters* (New York: Macmillan, 1956), p. 107.

2. John Sherrill, *They Speak with Other Tongues* (Old Tappan, New Jersey: Fleming H. Revell Company, Spire Edition, 1964).

Your Personal Notes

Your Personal Notes

For a free copy of Aglow Magazine and a catalog of other Aglow publications write to:

Aglow Publications
7715 - 236th SW
Edmonds, WA 98020